(out of print) $7.00
—————
66

1079

D1075140

FAITH FOR LIVING

BOOKS BY LEWIS MUMFORD

Faith for Living

LEWIS MUMFORD

HARCOURT, BRACE AND COMPANY   NEW YORK

Typography by Robert Josephy

PRINTED IN THE UNITED STATES OF AMERICA

BY QUINN & BODEN COMPANY, INC., RAHWAY, N. J.

"Faith for Living" begins at the point where "Men Must Act" left off. That book examined the cancerous nature of fascism and proposed an immediate policy for limiting its rapid spread into what still seemed healthy tissue. I must assume that the reader has read "Men Must Act" or will turn to it for further confirmation. Otherwise it may seem that in the present work I have taken too much for granted. "Faith for Living," however, turns to more ultimate issues.

"Men Must Act" appeared two years too early. Its words fell upon deaf ears and upon minds too comfortably padded, too nicely poised, too smugly self-assured, to be capable of timely action. "Faith for Living" has just the opposite defect: it appears twenty years too late. Even those who share its faith, or are belatedly converted to it, may be dead before they can make their beliefs fully manifest. At best, this book is a testament for survivors, if ever they reach shore.

What I have uttered is, I hope, no private faith; certainly it is no original one. I but remind the reader of those durable ideals of life which in the past have kept humanity going during its most anguished and shattered moments. Forgetfulness of these ideals has helped to bring on the very catastrophe we must now live through; remembrance of them may help us to survive it.

—L. M.

In composing "Faith for Living" I have drawn on various older writings: in particular, "What I Believe" (*The Forum*, November 1930), "The Social Responsibilities of Teachers" (*The Educational Record*, October 1939), "The Corruption of Liberalism" (*The New Republic*, April 29, 1940), and two unpublished lectures delivered in Honolulu, Hawaii, under the auspices of the Progressive Education Association, in June 1938. But the major part of the book appears now for the first time.

CONTENTS

viii

PART ONE:

The Betrayal of Man

> . . . Arts are tools;
> But tools, they say, are to the strong:
> Is Satan weak? Weak is the wrong?
> No blessed augury overrules:
> Your arts advance in faith's decay:
> You are but drilling the new Hun
> Whose growl even now can some dismay;
> Vindictive in his heart of hearts,
> He schools him in your mines and marts—
> A skilled destroyer.
>
> HERMAN MELVILLE

1. NO FLIGHT FROM THE WRATH TO COME

Today every human being is living through an apocalypse of violence. Fear enters the door with the daily newspaper, and the last radio report in the evening creates a waking nightmare which slips unnoticed into the horrors of sleep. Even the most miserable beggar, during the lazy stretch of the Victorian peace, had more security in his life and better chance of escaping rancorous violence than those who now command fortunes and great enterprises. Terror and misery have never stalked through the world on this scale, sparing no people, by-passing no country, since the Black Plague swept over Europe in the fourteenth century.

The question that confronts every man, woman, and child is how long they can stand this misery, and what powers do they have for survival? Will we endure? Will our civilization endure? What effort must we put forward to escape the refined degradations and the diabolical enslavements that the universal triumph of fascism would ensure for us? What false pride must we sacrifice in order to restore to ourselves the powers of action? At what point will we stand and face the enemy, not with arms alone, but with that overwhelming internal unity and conviction

3

which will ensure a sufficient supply of arms, and with this, the resolution to use them?

Now, for the first time in human history there is no spot on earth where the innocent may find refuge. No ark will keep us afloat; no Bamboo Grove, where philosophers might meditate, is immune from the barbarian's bombs; no foreign land is itself free enough from the threat of oppression to give safety to the oppressed. And no havens of refuge exist, like the monasteries of the Dark Ages, which the barbarians would respect. Since the rise of fascism, violence has become unqualified and universal; and it is civilization itself—not this or that patch of civilization—that is threatened with ruin.

Those of us who were children before 1914, even those who had reached manhood before 1933, were brought up in a relatively innocent world: a world that did not for a moment suspect that sweetness and light were not left behind automatically in the wake of the telephone, the steamship, and the airplane.

We certainly did not believe, as Fourier had suggested, that the very ocean would some day turn into lemonade, in proof of human harmony and amity. But we were quite as well prepared to see it turn into lemonade as we were prepared for the actual developments that have followed the rise of fascism, particularly in its open, virulent phase. It was easier to conceive of a series of chemical changes that might convert salt water into sweetened citric acid, than to conceive that human beings, with eyes, ears, hands, dimensions, machines, like our own might deliberately transform themselves into barbarians.

I shall not exaggerate our innocence in the recent past, up to 1914, or even until 1933. It is only by comparison with the present world that the past can be regarded as happy or untroubled. Very grave evils naturally existed. On the personal side, there were cheating, theft, bribery, assaults, rapes, murders, sins and mortal accidents of all kinds. Daniel Webster's proud boast about the Massachusetts of his day, that it was so free of crime that no country householder need lock his door at night, no longer held true even in Massachusetts. But for a century men had dreamed of making worldwide a peace and security that had once been maintained only in the ancient Roman Empire. Particularly after the first World War, with its ten million dead, there was genuine revulsion against the systematic, collective violence of war. For the mass of mankind, war had become an unthinkable obscenity, like eating the human body.

Humanity's deep sense of outrage expressed itself for the greater part, unfortunately, in a sort of negative pacifism: a desire to disarm and be quit of the instruments of war. This was abetted by a feeling of guilt that spread through the countries that had imposed the Treaty of Versailles upon the German people. So innocent was this world that no one guessed, in the mood of repentance, that the fascist barbarians who rose to power in Germany in 1933 would commit more horrible injustices and more unmentionable injuries in twelve months than the governing classes of England and France had succeeded in doing in as many decades.

But at the moment war became an absolute evil to most men, it became an absolute good for the new barbarians: that conjuncture was to prove disastrous. The barbarians were ready to sacrifice co-operations and understandings that men had been building up for centuries, in order to wreak their vengeance upon a civilization that regarded lawless collective violence as an ultimate stigma of human degradation.

Need I dwell on the consequences we face today? The innocent world that existed before 1933 is gone. That false sense of security has vanished completely. We realize at last that our mistake was a radical one, which showed we had not interpreted man's history well enough to understand either our own society or the nature of the human personality. We had glibly assumed that barbarism was a condition that civilized man had left permanently behind him: that certain kinds of cruelty, certain kinds of bestiality and violence, could never occur on a large scale again. We did not realize that in each generation man must reconquer the Yahoo within him, and re-establish his own right to be human.

The eruption of barbarism has not merely shown that

6

raw nature, gnawing at the heart of man, can encompass cruelties that rival the blind fury of the hurricane and the earthquake and the volcanic upheaval. Something else has been disclosed to our unwary eyes: the rottenness of our civilization itself. This structure, which seemed so solid, has been battered and shattered by a relatively small number of fanatical men. The combined forces of civilized people might have sufficed almost any time before 1940 to cripple the powers of fascism, had they been brought together with anything like the concentration of purpose that fascism showed. So that if our civilization should perish, this would come about, in part, because it was not good enough to survive. For what are all our fine instruments for rapid communication, if we do not use them to communicate intelligence and to unite and equip the civilized? Barbarism has used every modern instrument to destroy the peoples who had put too much confidence in the instruments by themselves, without fortifying and enlarging the spirit behind them. But this is to anticipate.

2. THE ILLUSION OF SECURITY

One of the greatest handicaps in facing the realities of the present world is that people have thought that progress was automatic, and that the special forms of life we had worked out in the last two centuries were permanent. Any other mode of feeling and acting was, to them, unthinkable—and therefore, despite the growing evidence of their senses, non-existent. For people do not believe in what they see unless the things they see correspond to what they believe.

There were reasons for this smugness. If a generation ago one had gazed only at the surface of modern society one might well have thought that its forms were permanent. (The Romans themselves had this illusion about their empire as late as the fifth century A.D., when its ruins were falling in clouds of dust and debris at their feet.) Many schemes of reform were abroad: even a revolutionary workers' movement that aimed to establish a commonwealth in which labor would be supreme, and its entire fruits would go to the laborer. But no matter how radical these plans, they all supposed more or less that the structure would hold together.

Like Roman society, capitalism had brought a certain

unity and order to every part of the planet. One might be sure of the same cocktails in Shanghai as in Paris. On trains that ran from Paris to Constantinople or from St. Petersburg to Vladivostok, the same International Sleeping Car cockney was spoken by the stewards, with varying national accents. If, before 1914, one took out insurance in Boston, its risk might be shared through the services of a broker in Brussels between a company in Moscow and one in Vienna. A traveler who avoided a few exceptional countries ruled by despotic governments—Russia and Turkey were the chief offenders—could steam over the world without a passport: "safe as a child" as one used to say, before fascism made that usage ironical.

The material structure of that world collapsed after the first World War, in the period of expropriation, inflation, military suspicion, and nationalistic isolation which infected almost every country. But the friendships, partnerships, understandings it had promoted have vanished even more completely. Difficulties of language and idiom, which obstructed co-operation in the past, were presently increased by more formidable barriers: differences in ideology and outlook which make rational intercourse impossible.

Plainly one cannot argue with a communist who refers to Russia's assault upon the Finns as a capitalistic conspiracy on the part of less than four million people to wipe out the so-called communism of one hundred sixty million or more people. Such language makes sense only in a madhouse. Neither can one come to terms with a Nazi when he uses the word "peace" to describe unobstructed conquest on the part of his party and nation, and the word "war-monger" to stigmatize anyone who seeks to oppose that conquest. On such a basis of non-truth and non-communication, one can not even express rationally the differences that exist among people of good will and common honesty.

In many areas the habits and ways of the early twentieth century are farther away from us than those of a thousand years ago. So great is the gap, the difference cannot be measured in years. William Morris, in his "News from Nowhere," thought that the people in his utopia of the future might read the novels of the nineteenth century in order that the miseries recorded in them might spice the flat happiness of their too perfect lives. Miseries and troubles indeed! If one turned to the closing days of the nineteenth century now, it would be for another reason—to recapture an incredible idyll of human felicity.

In those days the young might hope to leave their nonage behind without encountering, except in a chance newspaper story, even the faint shadow of that purposive brutality from which the world now cowers and shrinks. The voice of the German Kaiser Wilhelm, urging the German soldiers at Peking to emulate the Huns in frightfulness, sounded like the shriek of a maniac from some forgotten dungeon. At the end of the nineteenth century France was shaken to the roots by a single act of injustice done to a Frenchman who was also a Jew, Captain Dreyfus: more shaken by the Dreyfus affair than the whole world permits itself to be today, in the face of the colossal acts of violence and vengeance fascism wreaks on its victims, not on a single man, but on whole races, classes, nations, numbering millions.

Looking back to the nineteenth century for comparison, we see that the molehills of evil that then existed have, through fascism, become veritable mountains. The sinful men and women in the pages of Tolstoy, Zola, or Proust seem virtually angels alongside the sub-men that Nazism has fashioned. It is only in Dostoyevsky that one has a vista of the infernal depths to which the fascists have collectively sunk. Today Raskolnikov and Stavrogin march in goosestep; their name is legion; and their heels are everywhere, particularly on the prone bodies of the weak and the innocent.

To regard all this violence as primarily the symptom of economic maladjustment is a perversion of good sense. The gangster who controls a policy racket does not build up an army of gunmen and create a vast machine for extracting loot merely because he has not been given the chance to earn his living as a grocery clerk. He denies the value of the grocery clerk's sober useful life; he would spurn to manage even a chain of groceries, unless they promised some of the coarse drama and swagger he achieves as a racketeer.

So with fascism: it exists, not because the treaty of Versailles ladled reparations out of Germany so long as foreign investors enriched Germany permanently by pouring capital back; nor does it exist because, at the end of this fantastic period of economic illusions, a depression hit the whole world. The people of the United States experienced a far heavier economic drop between 1930 and 1935 than the Germans did before Hitler got into power; but our country did not become fascist. Why? The essential explanation for this difference is not an economic one: it is psychological and moral: the denial by the fascists of the positive values by which civilized men have always sought to live. This denial was built on a national tradition that goes back to Fichte and Luther in Germany, to Machiavelli and the Renaissance despots in Italy.

By 1930 the moral cement that heretofore held democratic Western society together had disappeared. This fact gave the fascist his opportunity: it abetted his own strength and it weakened the resistance of his victims. In short, a twofold demoralization.

3. INNER DECAY COMES FIRST

One of the great difficulties in understanding what has taken place under our eyes, dismantling our seemingly stable world order, is the fact that political and economic disturbances are usually the final symptoms of a collapsing civilization. These visible facts are preceded by a much longer period of inner decay, which only a few people—usually separated from their society by alien beliefs—recognize as the symptom of organic disease.

In the case of the Roman Empire, it is easy to see the weakness of our habit of looking for physical symptoms first, instead of understanding that in society matter and spirit never exist except in close partnership. Now spirit, by reason of its sensitivity, may record transformations that are invisible to the naked eye: just as pain or languor may indicate a disturbance in the body long before a malady defines itself in more observable deteriorations of tissue.

From the third century A.D. on, a whole host of economic and political difficulties became visible to the historian, following the period of peace and prosperity and effective government under the Antonine emperors. The rising burden of taxes, the infiltration of barbarians into the army,

13

the appearance of military dictatorships, the deforestation of Italy and Dalmatia, the lapse of agriculture under serfdom—all these and other forces were active. They are often treated as the prime causes of Rome's downfall.

But unfortunately for this mode of explanation, the actual disintegration of the Roman world had been going on for a much longer period. Intellectually, Rome had been living off the leavings of Greek culture; and from the second century B.C. onward the Greeks themselves had ceased to be really vital carriers of their own tradition; for their work was no longer supported by the activities of free citizens, aiming at the best life possible. They no longer had control over their own destinies.

Roman sculptors could copy the Greeks, as Roman philosophers could write glosses and comments on Plato, Aristotle, and Epicurus; but the impulse to create art presently dwindled into the mere connoisseurship of Pausanias. They acquired their culture, these Romans, on Samuel Butler's theory that it is cheaper to buy milk than to keep a cow. But by that fact they were unable to produce any milk of their own when the dairy went out of business. To make up for this, the Romans first watered the milk; then they sought by quick purchase to open up other supplies: now in Egypt, now Persia, now Palestine. This culture shopping only hastened the decay. Grabbing at the forms and meanings of every surrounding society, the Romans literally failed to hold their own.

All this happened long before the major physical crises appeared. It produced a sense of malaise that afflicted the prosperous and the powerful, quite as much as it touched the enslaved and the subjugated. Rome fell ultimately because from at least the first century on people ceased to believe in it. All the duties, obligations, and sacrifices that are demanded by a living society, especially in its early moments of adversity, came to seem burdensome. Accustomed to live on slave labor, as we have lived on the machine, the Romans lost their capacity for self-help; and ultimately they were at the mercy of their barbarian hirelings.

What was worse, the whole routine of this society came to seem trivial and unimportant to a growing body of people. Even its pleasures tasted sour. Gibbon, following many Roman sophists, attributed the débâcle to Christianity; but this obviously does not answer the critical question: Why did the proud Romans become Christians?

Those who believe that comforts and luxuries are the chief end of man will have difficulty in explaining why the distaste for them began to grow precisely at the moment when they were distributed with a lavish hand to the whole population. The explanation was not sour grapes; the grapes were within reach, for anyone's plucking. In every city the populace had luxurious baths. Yet decent people began to sicken at the very sight of the naked body, coddling itself in the midst of monumental luxury, in con-

15

tact with a thousand other naked bodies. There were circuses, where men were killed for human excitement, even as motor racers are killed for popular thrills today. But a growing body of people felt degraded every time they took part in these spectacles. Bread and circuses and baths were free to all; pure water flowed into the cities and sewage flowed out of them: a triumph of hygiene and sanitation. And yet—

And yet life itself did not keep sweet. There was starvation in the midst of plenty. People asked for bread and unfortunately all they got was bread: as if man could live by bread alone. Bored, surfeited, people looked about them for a religion that would have some meaning for them, and for a leader, a savior, a god, who would restore them to real life. Long before the material shell of this empire had collapsed, hundreds of thousands of Christians and Manicheans had renounced its supposed advantages, had condemned its boasted habits of life, and had deliberately given away their fortunes and reduced all their personal comforts—sometimes to the point of inflicting painful penances on themselves.

A similar renunciation, a similar act of sacrifice, might have kept the Roman Empire going indefinitely, if the ruling classes could have mustered the faith that would have enabled them to make it. Had the Romans been as selfless as the Christians were, they might have stoutly carried on their old selves. But the humility and the faith that would have made this possible disappeared after Marcus Aurelius, if not long before. So the shell collapsed, since the spirit no longer collaborated in its support.

For this same reason, our own civilization is now already partly in ruin, and large areas are occupied by barbarians more ruthless than Attila or the Vandal chiefs. Let us not be deceived by outward signs of activity and vitality. In the very generation that Rome finally fell into the hands of the barbarians, there were renewed expenditures, on a grand scale, for public works.

4. THE UNEARNED INCREMENT OF RELIGION

During the last century in the Western World, the aggrandizement of the machine and the degradation of man went hand in hand. Yet the moral energies which had accumulated in Western Europe in the course of twenty-five hundred years or more did not immediately die out. Just the opposite of this happened. Though the institutional forms of religion dried up, and for a large part of the population became, in the eighteenth century, a mere husk of habit, the inner aroma of Jewish morals and Christian belief pervaded the air of the Enlightenment. Indeed, the embers burned with fierce brightness, in a Wesley, an Elias Hicks, a Leo Tolstoy, before they finally mingled with the ashes of a cold hearth.

Out of the religious belief in a universal order, pervading the entire cosmos, came the confidence to abandon soothsaying and divination, and to formulate that order through the systematic observation of nature: modern science. Out of the belief in the absolute equality of souls before God came the belief in the equal social worth of all men, regardless of their talent, their ancestry, or their inherited privileges: the essence of democracy. Out of a belief in the perfectibility of the human soul, which car-

18

ried with it the promise, so often uttered by the Jewish prophets, of a heaven upon earth, came the generous utopianism of the eighteenth century, with its vision of a united humanity, released from stale privileges, provincial falsehoods, and inhuman degradations.

The theologian's Heaven took new form as the secular thinker's Future. With this came the belief in a social order governed by human need, adjusted to human capacity, in which society itself would become a collective work of art. To each according to his needs, from each according to his ability: here, in Jeremy Bentham's words, was the pledge of a larger justice than that which had hitherto prevailed. This doctrine was incorporated in nineteenth century socialism.

What were liberty and democracy, ultimately, but the moral belief in the freedom of the will and in man's capacity to make moral choices, governed by reason: a doctrine far older than St. Thomas Aquinas, who expressed it with classic distinction. And what indeed was the humanitarianism that so deeply distinguished the last century and a half but an effort to gentle the raw brutalities of the world on the Christian assumption that kindness will awaken kindness, and pity will breed remorse? Toward the criminal, the insane, the diseased, and the helpless, the humanitarian ethic re-established the old Christian attitude: compassionate understanding. Despite a thousand shortcomings in the economic order, the sense of human brotherhood visibly widened.

One might say, without paradox, that Christianity was never so strong in the Western World as at the moment when it was disappearing from the active consciousness of the more educated groups. Despite many counter-currents, many residual evils and not a few new ones, there was probably more of the active spirit and impetus of Christianity at work in the nineteenth century than had existed at any time since the twelfth century. The meek had not yet inherited the earth; but at least they had a hope and a prospect of coming into that inheritance.

What seemed on the surface a movement in life and thought that had no religious affiliations, sometimes even denied them, turns out on analysis to be the final flowering of fifteen centuries of religious and moral culture. Meanwhile, this religious culture had itself been undergoing a long disintegration, the causes of which I shall presently examine. But the perfume of a humane doctrine floated on the air: for a while it acted as a comforting hypnotic, which caused men to lose the sense of what had been lost, or to undertake the efforts necessary to make that loss good. People who no longer went to Church, or who, if they did, rejected many of its plainly moribund doctrines, like physical hellfire and eternal damnation for the unbaptized—such people attributed to natural human goodness what was actually the survival of a strong ethic and a deliberate discipline.

In short, the twentieth century inherited a morality which it had never worked for, which it had never examined and criticized and assimilated, which it was incapable of reproducing in fresh forms that could be handed on to its children. The husk of religion remained; but the precious life in its germ lacked a soil in which it could grow. Religion ceased gradually to be a social force and became a private idiosyncrasy; or rather, where it was most active and positive as a social force it tied itself, not to the interests of the poor and lowly, but to the profits of those who governed them. Christianity was not practical in this new society: so practice was only in the rare instance Christlike. There was perhaps a closer unity between faith and act among the Jews and the Mohammedans: but wherever modern industrial society was strongest, the hypocrisies and dissimulations of the pious expanded.

The humanitarian clouds of the eighteenth century, colored by its hopes for justice and human brotherhood, floated away: on the earth beneath lay exposed the cold programs of mechanical progress, as the end of ends and the purpose of purposes. The final result of this was a life without ethical content or ideal purpose: a life ready to shrivel into nothingness at the first whiff of fascism's poison gas. Those who had lived for so long on the unearned increment of religion were unable, like most *ren-*

tiers, to support themselves by their own independent efforts. So it came about that the main business of religion, in the period of industrial progress, was not to change life's direction but to slacken its pace. Religion retarded some of the worst developments, perhaps, along with some of the best. But it did not forthrightly oppose them; still less did it dare to do what the Christian Church had to some extent done all through the Dark Ages—throw its weight in the opposite direction.

All this is merely to say that the power of institutional religion had almost vanished. Its place was taken by the religion of power. Let us examine the features of this new creed; for it is the last grizzled, pock-eaten, warped, dehumanized visage of the power personality that now parades before the world as fascist youth.

5. THE THREEFOLD CULT OF POWER

Fascism is a deliberate reversion to the primitive: it is an organized revolt against civilization itself. Hence it cuts itself off from the emotional faith of Christianity, which goes back to Judaea, and from the free intellectual traditions of liberalism, which reach back to ancient Greece. Is this reversion to the primitive an accidental fact, due to infantile tendencies in the leaders of this new cult? Or is it perhaps an effort to counterbalance an equally perverse overemphasis of the impersonal, the dehumanized, in short the mechanical?

Before one can answer this question one must recall the origins of the machine. Most studies of industrial society up to very recently have ignored the long germinal period that preceded the modern cult of the machine. They have been preoccupied with the more obvious results of mechanical discipline, with inventions, labor-saving devices, scientific discoveries, and the like; just as if any of these things could have come into existence in a society that found its daily food dropping from the banana, the mango, or the palm tree, any more than they could have in the amiable culture of China, where gunpowder was originally used only to make harmless violent noises at festivals.

The fact is that the mechanical inventions of the eighteenth century happened after a long period of preparation. The soil in which they grew had been systematically cultivated by two great institutions: militarism and capitalism. All three institutions sprang out of a central impulse in the human personality: the desire to expand power, even at a ruthless sacrifice of life itself. This involves a willingness to renounce activities, to limit capacities, to forfeit human joys and delights that do not lead indirectly or directly to the achievement of power. Power over the forces of nature: power over time and space: power over the activities of other men.

That impulse in some sense is a primordial one. We are all children of the sun, and only by capturing the energy of the sun, only by converting sunlight into food, food into our own flesh and blood, can we have life on any terms. Even the leanest ascetic requires some slight fundament of this power; and in the subjective exercise of power, holding a plow, shooting a gun, swimming in the water, driving a car, is a deep pool of delight that testifies to something that is more than mere brute satisfaction. For man's command of power immensely increases his vitality.

But the higher cultures have usually bridled the exorbitant will-to-power that exists in man: they have sought for a fuller and more deeply sustained kind of human de-

velopment. Power, it always seems, runs the danger of becoming anti-human, turning against itself like that horrible creature in Dante's Inferno who feeds on his own
flesh. When the power impulse dominates life it shrivels
all the generous domestic instincts that ensure the race's
survival, since in so far as man is still an animal, he is,
at bottom, a domesticated animal; and the chief specimen
of his art is himself.

Capitalism as it developed became a comprehensive system of ideas, almost a religion. In fact, in its first cru-
sading phase, it tended to supplant Christianity as a practical working religion; and the virtues it preached—honesty,
abstention from idle amusements, thrift—took to themselves an extra sanctity derived from religion itself. As a
result of this one-sided concentration on the symbols of
power and the means of power, capitalism tended to displace the values of art, religion, friendship, parenthood.
These goods, the only goods that the poor majority of mankind had ever securely called their own, were despised and
belittled.

Nothing was good in a capitalistic sense unless it could
be produced by organized enterprise, unless it could be
sold at a profit, unless a part of these profits could be set
aside—and this was a first consideration, along with the
accumulation of capital itself—as a means of supporting
a group of people called *rentiers*, or investors, in a state

of economic idleness. As soon as profits ceased to be produced, the wheels stopped moving, no matter how desperate the need for the commodity. To go on otherwise, on
business terms, was to court bankruptcy.

The sort of life that is made possible in the tropical
isles of the Pacific through the bounties of nature, through
an almost playful round of labor—this sort of life was
from the standpoint of pure capitalism little less than
sacrilege. It involved too little effort, and, above all, it
promised no profit, despite the fact that the natives, thanks
to nature, were in the position of the favored leisure classes
of capitalistic civilization.

Balzac pictured the rapacious impulses behind capitalism a century ago in all their wolflike nakedness; and the
final results of its ethic and its vision of life are now mani-
festing themselves in the worldwide betrayal of modern
civilization by those who put economic gain before the
safety and liberty of their fellow-countrymen. In the cur-
rish behavior of the "two hundred families" of France,
in the betrayal by the class that the Birmingham business
man, Chamberlain, represented, one witnesses the manner
in which avarice becomes in effect if not in intention treason. The Dutch capitalists who sought to keep the wealth
of the Indies without even the life-insurance policy of pro-
viding modern armaments, show how fatuous and feeble
capitalism becomes through its very preoccupations. No

wonder these financiers awaken the Nazis' contempt: they deserve it.

Do not misunderstand my meaning: this is only one side of the ledger, the debit side. Like every other institution that has a long history, capitalism had a real reason for existence, and it had a powerful contribution to make to human culture. For capitalism produced the orderly, the methodical man: it made universal an almost ascetic type of personality that had hitherto appeared only among those of a more saintly disposition who had been disposed to shake off the claims of this world. Capitalism therefore vulgarized some of these essential virtues and acclimated them to secular life. The Quaker and the Parsee, in whom this religious connection is most plain, more often than not became the outstanding business men of their respective communities: the hard-shell Baptist virtues of the original Mr. Rockefeller offer another example.

Capitalism, by its careful accountancy of money, laid the foundation for accurate, quantitative notions about everything else in the universe. Habit and guesswork were displaced by systematic calculation, orderly analysis, planful activity: the day was divided, the hours carefully accounted for, the time-schedule introduced, and every minute watched. Capitalism thus provided one of the large ingredients of the scientific mind; and it is no accident that the bankers and big merchants of London were among the earliest experimenters in the Royal Society, or that a simi-

27

lar group in Philadelphia founded under Franklin a kindred institution, the American Philosophical Society.

If we save our civilization from the barbarian, we shall also save all that is valuable in capitalism, including the original sense of initiative and experiment it introduced into the world.

6. MANUFACTURING SOLDIERS AND ROBOTS

No less important than capitalism in the development of our machine civilization was another element that is usually not thought of immediately: the modern army, and the militaristic habits of mind that have developed out of it.

Militarism was not merely responsible for early technological improvements like gunpowder and cannon; and it has not merely called upon the best scientific minds of the time, from Archimedes to Leonardo, for their contributions to its technics. In addition, militarism has been responsible, no less than the capitalistic bureaucracy, for popularizing the mechanical discipline of life and for regimenting body and mind.

The army, in fact, is the source of many types of uniformity and standardization that we ordinarily attribute to its steel successor, the automatic machine. Military drill, introduced into the army at the end of the sixteenth century, anticipated on the human level the automatism and the iron discipline of the factory. In the production of uniforms and equipment, made of standardized, replaceable parts, militarism paved the way for mass production in every other department of life. Whitney's guns and

Bentham's warships were the first to employ standard, identical, pre-fabricated parts.

Militarism helped to concentrate political authority in relatively small groups. In this it resembled the tendencies of capitalism. These armed groups had power of life and death over those who lacked equally deadly weapons for their protection: with the aid of his primitive muskets and implacable discipline the Western European overwhelmed primitive peoples who far outnumbered him. Militarism was thus in good part responsible not only for the loss of municipal freedom and autonomy in Western Europe, with a centralization of power in the great war-capitals; but also for the subjugation of Africa, America, and Asia. Cortez's conquest of Mexico was symbolic of the whole process. Unfortunately, the success of militarism was an achievement, not merely in mechanical efficiency, but in dehumanization.

We must rid our minds, then, of the notion that militarism and war are accidental eruptions in a fundamentally peaceful industrial civilization: that they are merely leftovers from an earlier state of violence, from whose savagery and disorder mechanical civilization has attempted to release us. This is a grotesque misreading of the facts. Militarism, on the contrary, has expanded with every expansion of the machine and in turn it has fostered that expansion.

And mark this: the spread of this autocratic discipline,

the manufacture of soldiers and robots, was not stayed by the rise of democracy. For it was the French Revolution that gave to military commanders that hitherto unknown instrument of power—the national army, obtained by universal conscription: the first step to total war. The effect of this change was progressively to inure almost every nation—the English and the Americans excepted—to military practices. Standardization, drill, automatic conformity spread everywhere.

The army became the school of the power-state; and the schools of the state became, in effect, armies. Unfortunately for the incidental educational process, the army is a bachelor institution as much as the monastery: the natural impulses of love, affection, tenderness, were excluded from its one-sided discipline: bad for the soldier's morale. This further deepened the essential barbarism of the process itself.

Here again, in gauging the results of the life-denying tendencies of military drill and automatism, which produce that characteristic occupational disease, the stupidity of the soldier, one does not seek to belittle militarism's real achievements. The element of inflexible discipline can obviously be overdone: often it has been blindly, viciously overdone on the parade ground, where mechanically perfect posture has deformed the body; in the bureaucracy, where it has sterilized the mind; and above all in the school.

But no good work in any sphere is ever carried through without a readiness, when the occasion demands, to submit to sacrifices, privations, pains, and even death: does not Androcles, in Shaw's play, face the tortures of the arena to uphold the honor of a tailor? And perfection in any art, even those arts whose final effects seem most spontaneous and released, can be obtained only by repeated and continued effort, often exacting, exhausting, inflexible, monotonous. The good dancer, the good musician, the good lover achieves the effect of creative spontaneity only because he is not satisfied with the result of his original awkward efforts or too easily pleased by his first indolent triumphs. There is an element of compulsive sacrifice in all the arts. This holds equally for the sciences.

In reacting against the brutal features of militarism the liberals and pacifists usually abandon as equally worthless the rational element in this discipline: in that they are wrong. Similarly, in reacting against that ultimate indignity to the spirit that springs out of wanton violence and the exaltation of untrammeled physical power, in contempt of reason and co-operative understanding, they forget that there are some convictions and ideals for which every man must be prepared to answer with his life.

In the soldier, courage is his essential virtue and the duty of facing death at any moment is a professional obligation—the most important element in his self-respect. A philosophy of life that confines this element to the soldier must prove too sickly to preserve either its joys or its liberties. Here is the higher side of militarism's drill and impersonality. It is the basis of the soldier's inherent contempt for the civilian, and above all for the prudent business man, who would buy his security with money, and who does not feel equipped to face the world without overshoes, umbrellas, life-insurance, and aspirin.

The counterpart of the soldier in the industrial world is the robot: the automatic machine or the worker who has himself become a cog in an impersonal automatic machine. The organization of men, machines, and natural sources of power into large integrated units has given man his almost godlike dominion over the forces of nature. At the same time it has left the individual human unit, whether he be a drudge on an assembly line or the head of a vast commercial enterprise, with an increasing sense of inferiority and impotence.

This ironic result recalls the words of Isaiah: they seem to ring across the centuries to the present generation. "Ye turn things upside down! Shall the potter be counted as clay; that the thing made should say of him that made it, He made me not; or the thing framed say of him that framed it, He hath no understanding?" Precisely this has happened in our topsy-turvy world.

As the industrial system becomes more rationalized,

more clock-like in its operations, the behavior of its members, as Karl Mannheim pointed out, becomes less and less voluntary, less and less subject to self-rule. When the alarm clock goes off, the worker rises; when the factory whistle blows, he goes to work; when the engines start up, he stands ready to watch the spindles or the shuttles, or to add his bolt or wheel to the machine that goes down the assembly line. Less power, less intelligence, less individual discretion falls to the lot of the individual worker. Even the farmer, with far more room to turn round in, still must be at the call of distant markets, if he is to provide for himself in return the goods those markets offer. Each life has its small part in an impersonal machine; and that machine is in turn part of a larger and remoter machine.

This is the fundamental regimentation of the modern world. It cannot be attributed to fascism; but on the contrary, the easy hold that fascism has taken can be partly laid to the fact that self-help and self-government and self-control have so largely disappeared from every department of our daily life. To punch the time clock, to stamp the slip, to o.k. the papers, to pass the buck, to go through certain external motions, without inquiry, without intelligent participation, has become the outstanding mark of our mechanical civilization.

Thinking, direction, intelligence has concentrated itself more and more at the top, while the subordinate jobs, whether they are those of a bookkeeper or an engineer or a salesman have become more impersonal, more mechanized, more irresponsible. This mechanization, as long as it works, makes ordinary men carefree: that is, in return for their exact devotions, they have the reward that all slaves have—their masters can do the worrying. Here, as Professor Geroid Tanquary Robinson has pointed out, is the very medium for despotism to flourish in.

7. THE PRIMITIVE AND THE PERSONAL

Slavery at the bottom, caprice at the top; mechanization at the bottom and raw savagery at the top: this is what modern society has come to. It is not due to the accidental rise of a Hitler or a Mussolini: it is rather the goal toward which the universal cult of power has driven us.

Those who have lost the very attributes of men will still, with what is left of their manhood, worship the first leader who exhibits them. Those whose jobs have become sterile and life-denying will seize the opportunity to feed the sources of their vitality, not with ordinary food, but with raw meat. They will scream because they have been permitted in their work only to whisper, or have been compelled to observe a Trappist silence. Silence! No smoking! Watch your step! Check out for the toilet!

So, too, they will worship great armaments, because they feel so powerless; they will bow to tribal gods, who demand blood and tribute, because the god within them is dead. They will give absolute freedom to their leader— trusting utterly his demonic inspirations or whims—because in that act they vicariously recover the normal sense of a free personality. They will be seized with delusions of grandeur, and fancy themselves blood brothers in a conquering race, because they themselves have been conquered.

In short: these victims of the machine will confirm their slavery in order to recover, at second hand, at least the illusion of freedom. This is, I believe, the psychological basis of fascism. Out of frustration come its grand aggressions: out of an inhuman mechanical discipline comes its more primitive assertion of humanity. Fascism has happened first in Russia, Italy, and Germany for a very simple reason: none of those countries had a long tradition of freedom. The despotism of the army and the machine erected itself on a political base that favored despotism. Serfdom was not finally abolished in Germany until the middle of the nineteenth century: that country had never undergone the sanative bath of a liberal revolution. Italy was governed by a succession of despots, in every principality and city, since the fifteenth century; whilst Russia had not even a dim memory of freedom: it was a word the educated had come across in English books. All these circumstances gave the initiative to countries whose very soil favored despotism, when the time came for the "faceless men" to make a religion out of the denial of life.

But the same facts which explain the rise of fascism in Germany and Italy also explain the lack of resistance in other countries. Men and women, industrial leaders and workers, the poor and even the rich, have all been subject to the same impersonal forces. But in Great Britain, France and the United States power in the form of money took precedence over power in the form of military weapons. And the cult of the primitive, in these countries, came back less in the forms of violence than in those of sensuous indolence and animal indulgence: in drunkenness and promiscuous sexuality and the paraphernalia of material wealth. These people are passive barbarians: no less than the more active ones that have produced fascism, they deny the values of mind and spirit, and renounce the discipline and the sacrifice that make men truly human.

In America we have created a new race, with healthy physiques, sometimes beautiful bodies, but empty minds: people who have accepted life as an alternation of meaningless routine with insignificant sensation. They deny because of their lack of experience that life has any other meanings or values or possibilities. At their best, these passive barbarians live on an innocent animal level: they sun-tan their bodies, sometimes at vast public bathing beaches, sometimes under a lamp. They dance, whirl, sway, in mild orgies of vacant sexuality, or they engage in more intimate felicities without a feeling, a sentiment, or an ultimate intention that a copulating cat would not equally share. They dress themselves carefully within the range of uniformity dictated by fashion. Their hair is curled by a machine; and what passes for thought or feeling is also achieved, passively, through the use of a machine: the radio or the moving picture today, or Aldous Huxley's "feelies" tomorrow.

These people eat, drink, marry, bear children and go to their grave in a state that is at best hilarious anesthesia, and at its worst is anxiety, fear, and envy, for lack of the necessary means to achieve the fashionable minimum of sensation. Without this minimum, their routine would be unbearable and their vacancy worse. Shopgirls and clerks, millionaires and mechanics, share the same underlying beliefs, engage in the same practices: they have a common contempt for life on any other level than that of animal satisfaction, animal vitality. Deprive them of this, and it is not worth living. Half dead in their work: half alive outside their work. This is their destiny. Every big city counts such people by the million; even the smaller provincial centers, imitating the luxury and the style of the big centers, with their fashion shows, night clubs, road houses, organized inanities, produce their full share of people equally empty of human standards and aims.

No small part of the cynicism that has eaten into this civilization is due to the triviality of its products and to the false excitement that attends their exploitation. A new brand of chewing gum! a new container for coffee! canned vitamins to achieve eternal youth! a new cigarette lighter! a streamlined toilet (to cut down wind resistance): scientific research that proves pepper is hot in the mouth or water is wet! An opulence of carefully packaged emptiness.

The novel and the newspaper accommodate themselves to the needs of these new barbarians; likewise the motion pictures. By endless repetition they build up a mental world that is free from any values except those of physical sensation and material wealth. This is a world in which business men become gangsters and gangsters become business men without changing a single essential habit in their lives: a world in which violence becomes normalized as part of the daily routine. The popular mind becomes softly inured to human degeneracy. "Tobacco Road" and "Of Mice and Men" become popular dramas without exciting the faintest degree of public protest— except in traditional clerical circles—over the defilement which they spread.

What such dramas portray doubtless exists. But the way in which they portray it shows that, for the writer and his public, for all their "good intentions" and "social interests," nothing else really exists. Murder, incest, adultery, sacrilege, have been the perpetual themes of human drama from Aeschylus to Shakespeare. What I challenge therefore is not the subject but the method and attitude. Only by a cleansing greatness of spirit, only by the sure possession of a scheme of ideal values, can a writer treat these subjects without degrading both himself and the spectator. Today this degradation is all but universal. No one is surprised when a gangster murders a man in the public thoroughfare; no one is surprised when a band of gangsters invade a peaceful country and put it under their "protection." People have seen it all before: they watch it passively, as they do the motion pictures. They count themselves lucky if they get a good snapshot of the murder or the invasion with their candid cameras.

It is on these passive barbarians, who have come to exist in great numbers even in countries that have free traditions, that the fascists have successfully relied in prosecuting their conquests. The people who turn their heads away when a Brown Shirt kicks a helpless old man in a public thoroughfare: the people who cower behind their doors when the Ogpu or the Gestapo rouses some poor victim at midnight to be taken to a concentration camp or shot in the back without going that far: the people who utter no word of protest against a regime that denies their humanity—people who dare not even vote No on a plebiscite, lest they be detected in that act: these are the passive supporters of fascism.

At best, there is lack of even animal courage among these passive barbarians; their chief motto is—*Don't stick out your neck!* At worst there is emptiness; a failure to feel their humanity challenged by cruelty, by violence, by despotism, by contempt for the weak and the helpless, by the spiteful renunciation of all the higher goods of moral-

41

ity, art, and science. Sometimes these barbarians by their passiveness pay off old resentments against a class or a people about whom they have real or imagined grievance; sometimes, as with many "communists," they pass over into the opposite camp, and renounce the very love of humanity as a whole which once stirred them to work everywhere for the exploited and the oppressed. So the tribes that were conquered by the Aztecs betrayed their masters to Cortez, only to suffer grievously in turn from the same conquest. That, too, has happened in our midst.

The more threatening the active barbarian's assault, the more inevitable becomes the passive barbarian's whine. "Why should we die in order to defend our country? Why shouldn't Hitler rule us, too? Maybe we'd be just as well off. What's freedom or democracy? Just words." Even now that whine, under the skillful shaping of fascist propaganda, is beginning to swell into a demand. Those who have already lost their manhood and their self-respect, who value their shabby little selves, regardless of what sort of life they pass on to their children, are the chosen accomplices of fascism: they are ready for its more boisterous denials of freedom, justice, and truth.

PART TWO:

Corruption of the Opposition

Therefore, since the world has still
Much good, but much less good than ill,
And while the sun and moon endure
Luck's a chance, but trouble's sure,
I'd face it as a wise man would,
And train for ill and not for good.

A. E. HOUSMAN

8. NEW WARS OF RELIGION

Fascism has swept over three countries, during the last dozen years, with the fanatical speed of a religion. The religion is a tribal one, and each of the tribes has its god, Mussolini, Stalin, and Hitler. In the case of Soviet Russia the change has taken place by infiltration and displacement: the original humanitarian and universal purposes have been leached out and an oriental despotism of very ancient type has occupied its old communist structure.

Each of these religions has made use of the machinery of modern life, as the Christian Church made use of the administrative mechanisms of the old Roman bureaucracy, and even borrowed the authority of the state in order to stamp out rival cults and heretical sects. Fascism has been helped in its conquests because it has thrown off the capitalist obsession of achieving power through the individual appropriation of money. This has given it a freedom to improvise financial arrangements of a breath-taking nature, from the standpoint of orthodox business, which assumes that if the necessary activities of a community cannot be sustained without profits, it is these activities, and not profits, that must be renounced.

In turn, however, fascism succumbs with massive fatal-

45

ity to the old feudal obsession with military power. Not
money, but planes, tanks, submarines, and mechanical
military equipment of all kinds—instruments of death—
become the supreme goal of all economic activity. With
the aid of these weapons the fascists, like the Romans of
old, propose to live by levying tribute off the peoples they
conquer and enslave. Those who are obsessed with money
cannot understand the fascist obsession with arms: the
purpose will not in fact dawn upon them until they learn
that fascism offers a crude alternative to its victims—Your
money and your freedom or your life.

Fascism is a diabolical religion, a religion of Yahoos:
that needs no demonstration today. But still it is a religion;
and this means that it has the capacity of every living religion to integrate action, to create a spirit of willing sacrifice, to conjure up in the community that possesses it a
sense of its collective destiny which makes the individual
life significant, even in the moment of death. Such a religion laughs at the business man's prudent calculations, or
at the valetudinarian ideal of prolonging all human life
to the age of three score and ten, in order that bridge-
whist players and golfers shall not lack experienced partners. And that mockery is deserved: Emerson said that life
was not worth having to do tricks in.

One cannot counter the religious faith of fascism unless
one possesses a faith equally strong, equally capable of
fostering devotion and loyalty, and commanding sacri-

fice. For a religion is a deep source of human energy and vitality; and no country can subdue this vitality in another people, or even head it off and keep its own life intact, by offering those who hold the religion a few paltry bribes, compromises, appeasements. No matter how tribal the fascist god may be, it is the very nature of a religion to tend toward universality: if it denies the brotherhood of man in peace and love and freedom, it will exact a kind of servile brotherhood from those whom it has conquered: they must participate in the cult as victims for the sacrifice and thus share the honors of the tribal altar with the high priest.

True: the converts to fascism are themselves in some sort victims. Behind all their rabid delight in the primitive lies a desire for death: this has its expression in the devotion to war. The Brown Shirts and Black Shirts mass to their death, shouting the name of their leader, with the same blind, fatal instinct that make the little lemmings fling themselves by thousands into the sea, to perish there by unaccountable mass suicide.

But the death impulse itself, so corruptly dynamic, calls for a life impulse as keen and unyielding in the forces that would oppose it. So the main problem of the present hour is this: Is there religion enough left in the mass of humanity to counteract the negative and diabolical religion that has swept to victory as fascism? What equivalent faith exists in the traditions of civilization to

47

oppose the collective psychosis that has seized the peoples of Germany and Italy and Japan and Russia and now threatens to dominate the world with barbaric fury, destroying all that it cannot understand?

Before we can summon up the deeper sources of our human tradition, we must examine the facile and routine beliefs that have been shared by liberals and traditionalists, by socialists and by tories, by agnostics and by the orthodox creeds. Why have they not in their own right been able to prevent the present crisis from arising? I do not undertake this examination to fix blame: I do so only that those of us who are not fascist in faith, may understand the weaknesses and deficiencies and sins that each of us has exhibited. The swift rise of fascism would not have been possible had there not been an incredible betrayal of the traditions of civilization itself: a betrayal by the very guardians of man's social heritage.

Fascism is the revenge that the barbarian visits upon the civilization that has not undertaken the burden of transforming Caliban into a docile agent of the human spirit. Not merely this: fascism also recalls certain obdurate truths about life itself which never entered the doctrines of those who believed in automatic progress. Indeed in the last easy century of middle-class philistinism, these truths tended to disappear even from the high religions, where they had once been firmly enthroned.

In the world today the traditional forces of civilization

include people of very diverse attitudes and performances. It is not practicable to define either the progressive tradition or the conservative tradition with any great delicacy of precision. But for the rough purposes of this argument, I shall group as traditionalists the great body of mankind that is united in the practice of any of the high religions: Christians, Jews, Mohammedans, Buddhists, Hindus, and Confucians.

These are the outstanding faiths. They all have their sources in a very remote past; and in spite of many lapses of faith, in spite of constant flouting, these religions still keep alive the tradition of man's divinity and high destiny. By contrast, the religion of Shintoism, as practiced in Japan, or the religion of Wotan, as practiced in Germany, openly or disguised as official Christianity, are low religions: they deny human brotherhood, and erect in place of a vision of perfection an idol of the tribe. In short, they remain at the stage that Judaism was in when it was only the local cult of Yahweh, as practiced by a tribe of fanatical herdsmen, fired by the notion of being the Chosen People. (Judaism outgrew that obsession: Nazism, hating the Jews, has fallen back into it and magnified it.)

The other body of beliefs is far more recent than the main stem of any of the traditional religions: it is based upon a faith in the perfectibility of man and his institutions, here on earth. But the tradition itself starts, as a self-conscious doctrine, with the Athenians: its basis is a faith in the human intelligence as a means of understanding nature and disciplining the human personality. The tradition of free inquiry in the modern mode starts with the Greeks. For them, nothing was sacred, in the sense of being outside the bound of free inquiry: they had theories about the constitution of matter, the physical nature of the earth, the proper form for political society, and what constitutes goodness, truth, and beauty. On the moral side, this heritage connects very closely with the Judaic tradition, which was contemporary with it, and the Christian tradition, which incorporated—though at first with misgiving—the very words Aristotle or Plato used to describe the ethical life.

The essential fact about free inquiry is freedom itself: a precious possession that the Athenians of the fifth century became acutely conscious of when faced with the surly provincialisms of the Spartans, and above all with the despotic Asiatic governments that threatened them. The Greeks perceived that a higher kind of life, alike from the moral and the intellectual and the political point of view, could not exist under despotism, where the thinker must not seek truth if the truth disturbs the political rulers, and where the moralist may not advocate any good which might threaten the advantages or privileges of the master group. I shall call this tradition ideal liberalism. Its recovery in the eighteenth century and its betrayal in our time constitute nothing less than a tragic drama.

Plainly, these bodies of belief are not entirely exclusive. Though the traditional religions have valued "goodness," godliness, or obedience to divinity more than they have usually valued intellectual inquiry, this emphasis is rather of recent date. Astronomy and the calendar go back to the religious cults of the Chaldeans; and every doctrine of Godhood has included as an essential part of God's manifestation a doctrine about the physical universe itself, the starry heavens and the earth beneath. In many religions, the sun itself is the deity or the deity takes on the virtues of the sun, just as the universal manifestations of life, reproduction, fertility, have their expression in Venus and Astarte, or their hardly less positive embodiment in Virgin Goddesses.

But in general, the traditionalists are backward-looking, conservative; pessimists about the future and optimists about the past. They seek the changeless and the immovable: the Eternal Yesterday, as Schiller says, which ever was and ever comes back again, and serves tomorrow because it served today.

The values of liberalism, except in sciences like astronomy and paleontology, are not rooted in any doctrine about the cosmos. Indeed they have rather been associated with the belittling notion, known to all men of science since the Greeks, and re-popularized by Galileo, that the earth is not the center of the universe, or even of the solar system. Liberalism, lacking any comfort from this cosmology, tends to fasten on the immediate scene. Its sense of time is keener for the future than for the past, partly because it regards the past as stupid and bad, and the future as hopeful, intelligent, and good.

Included in the broad main currents of liberalism are the shaping ideas of rational science, political democracy, and mechanical progress: this has been particularly true since the eighteenth century. Freedom in thought and expression: equality in political responsibility and power: improvement in the mechanical and social instruments of living—these tendencies have come together in modern liberalism. These ideas are partly continuations of the ideal traditions of liberalism; they are also in part—as I shall show—due to the fact that liberalism, being a little innocent and naive as to the nature of man, took over the cult of power without even suspecting the possibility of disastrous consequences.

In fine, the liberal keeps on hoping that progress will continue and that Utopia is just around the corner: whereas the traditionalist, just because he remembers better the ignominies of the past, assigns perfection to an after-life in Heaven. Even there he reserves it only for the elect.

Hardly ever are these bodies of belief exclusive: they overlap and mingle. A Seventh-Day Adventist may be an inventor; just as a scientist of high repute may have a touch of primitive magic left in him and avoid the cracks in the pavement when walking or knock wood when he boasts about his health. What one says about the liberals applies to many liberals, but not all; likewise to some conservatives. What one says about most conservatives, in relation to the institution of the Church, may also apply to many liberals, however atheistic, with regard to the home. In addition, both groups have grown up in the midst of a power civilization; so that no matter what their intellectual beliefs, their lives bear the stain and imprint of this environment. In some degree they are occupied with machines: in some degree they are affected by the habits and interests of the business man, or by the cult of military prowess.

Thus each of these religions is in some degree in conflict with the other. Those who valued political democracy found themselves a little while ago in opposition to those who sought political democracy only so long as it did not interfere with the political position of the Catholic Church in Spain. In addition, there are conflicts within each personality between the ideal aims and the life that is actually lived: often a disastrous contradiction.

Beneath these surface conflicts there are deeper and stubborner oppositions: conflicts between different visions of life, different world-pictures, as well as between different temperaments. This disharmony, this lack of unity, has been both a product of disintegration and a cause of it. Above all, it has led to a lack of intercourse between the two fundamental ideologies that could, if they were cleansed of their faults, hold the demonic geist of fascism in check. Christian universalism became tribal and parochial. Liberalism was in itself touched with the obsession of power: money, wealth, endless gadgets.

I purpose to examine this fatal lack of coherence and conviction in the main traditions of our civilization. These matters are glibly referred to in the Marxian demonology as the inherent contradictions of capitalism; and without doubt they have an economic base. But fascism has also sprung into existence in a society committed to socialism, Soviet Russia: hence the most serious difficulties must be dealt with on another plane—that of thought, belief, faith, or *Weltbild,* as the Germans put it.

9. THE DISINTEGRATION OF LIBERALISM

As a political doctrine liberalism was expressed in the English Revolution of 1642; in the American Revolution of 1776; and in the French Revolution of 1789: these three, and these three alone, produced permanent results on the character and temperament of the people, and became deeply embedded in all their ways and deeds and hopes. In each case, liberalism was an attempt to curb the irresponsible power and the hopeless inefficiency of despotism, once it had lost its first stern self-confidence.

As an economic doctrine, liberalism grew up in a world that sought to overcome the privileges and restrictions imposed by a paternal government upon industry: to scale down the burden of taxes whose main use was to increase the perquisites of flunkeys and enlarge the domains of courtiers. Liberalism here began as a creed of laissez-faire; but all the tendencies that were vital in it were concerned with the economic improvement of the lot of the common man, and when this did not come through laissez-faire liberalism shifted its tactic: so it debouched into the twentieth century as the party of collectivism and socialization.

Though capitalism has been the dominating force in our

society for more than a century, it has never presented a wholly united front, and it has never quite succeeded in imposing its doctrines on every class and group in the community. Despite lures, bribes, attractions, the great mass of mankind works for a living, not for profit. Wars and economic crises have shaken society; but precisely because of its mixed nature, its varied motives and means, its many survivals of more primitive economies, it has shown a resilience that contrasts favorably, at least in times of peace, with totalitarian regimes. Its worst mistakes result in bankruptcy or unemployment: whereas in the totalitarian economies, purges are the penalty for miscalculations and concentration camps the guarantee of order and unanimity between the conflicting parts of the economic organization.

The worst weakness of liberalism, on the economic side, derives from the very nature of our power culture; and I shall return to this at another point. But an even more serious failure, in some ways, lies on the personal and social side; for here the philosophy of liberalism has been dissolving before our eyes during the last decade: too noble to surrender, too sick to fight.

The liberal has begun to lack confidence in himself and in the validity of his ideals. In every country where the attacks on liberalism have been forceful, he has shown either that he does not possess stable convictions, or that he lacks the courage and the insight to defend them. Con-

tinually hoping for the best, the liberal has a total incapacity to face the worst; and on the brink of what may be
another Dark Age, he continues to scan the horizon for
signs of dawn. Facing a war waged mercilessly by fascism against all his ideals and hopes, the liberal shows
himself more concerned over minor curtailments of private liberties, necessary for an effective defense against
fascism, than he is over the far more ghastly prospect of
permanent servitude if fascism finally covers the earth.

Unable to take the measure of our present catastrophe,
and unable because of their inner doubts and contradictions and subtleties to make effective decisions, liberals
have lost most of their essential convictions: for ideals remain real only when one continues to realize them. The
record of the English laborites before 1940 is not better
than that of the Tories: the record of the Blums in France
is almost as disgraceful as that of the Bonnets. In the past
two decades liberals no longer acted as if justice mattered, as if truth mattered, as if right mattered.

The truth is the liberals no longer dared to act. In
America, during the period of the United Front, the liberals accepted the leadership of a small communist minority, fanatical, unscrupulous, deeply contemptuous of
essential human values, incredibly stupid in tactics and
incredibly arrogant in matters of intellectual belief; they
accepted this leadership simply because the communists,
alone among the political groups, had firm convictions

and the courage to act on them. How did this weakness develop? How did this betrayal come about?

The Romans used to say that the worst results come about through the corruption of what is good. One may say this about the present state of liberalism. But the defects of liberalism are not due to isolated mistakes of judgment that individual liberals have made. They are due to fatal deficiencies that go to the very root of the liberal philosophy. If we are to save the human core of liberalism—and it is one of the most precious parts of the entire human heritage—we must slough off the morbid growths that now surround it.

10. OUTER ASSAULT: INNER BETRAYAL

Like democracy, with which it has close historic affiliations, liberalism during the last generation has been the object of violent attack. This came originally from the Marxian revolutionaries of the left; but the blows have been doubled through the far more universal and triumphant actions of the fascist revolutionaries of the right. By now these extremes have met in their attacks upon liberalism. For all practical purposes, the despotic totalitarian systems, no matter how different their origins and basic ideals, cannot now be separated. Only minor theological differences still exist between a Father Coughlin and an Earl Browder, between a Mussolini and a Stalin.

According to the Marxian critics, liberalism arose at the same time as capitalism; and therefore liberalism is doomed to disappear when capitalism collapses by its own weight or is overthrown by the proletariat it develops. From the Marxian point of view, ideas are but the shadows of existing economic institutions and class stratifications. Human liberty depended upon freedom of investment, freedom of trade: liberty itself was merely a slogan that served the bourgeoisie in its rise to power. One might think, to hear many Marxian critics—Marx and Engels

usually avoided the mistake—that the concept of freedom had never been framed or the condition itself never
enjoyed before the Manchester school came into existence.

In truth, freedom derives from the essential human
capacity for self-determination and voluntary co-operation: self-help and mutual aid. On this point, the Scotch
moralist, Adam Smith, and the great Russian moralist,
Peter Kropotkin, were much sounder than Marx, who possessed more than a small share of that combination of
arrogance and authoritarianism which marks the mind of
Hegel. In short, Marx was a German, and only a handful of German thinkers have ever had even a glimmer of
the meaning of freedom. That is the sociological, if not
the economic determinist, explanation of Marx's disastrous
limitations as a universal thinker.

Freedom, in actuality, has been developed by steady
culture, by rational training, over thousands of years:
the Swiss have known it as farmers and dairymen and
clockmakers, the Dutch have known it as sailors and merchants, as the Greeks knew it before them in their day.
The necessity for freedom can be understood only by people who have a grasp of the self itself—or at least that
elemental sense of self-respect which even the poor and
unlettered may proudly bear. Many of my Dutchess
County farmer neighbors know what freedom is far better than the academic philosophers and political theo-
rists who have conformed too prudently to the conditions

outside them: who do not dare throw down a mean job or resent a degrading condition. Freedom is the very condition of that personal growth which distinguishes human society from a far superior type of social organization, that of the beehive or the anthill.

So the anti-liberals, pretending mainly to attack capitalism, have also attacked the belief in the worth and dignity of the individual personality, by asserting that it is bound up with capitalism. They have thus undermined the notion of a humanity that extends beyond race, class, creed, or other boundaries. The Nazis deny common humanity beneath differences of race, though their own conception of race has only spurious scientific foundations; whereas the communists deny it to class and creed —hence the capacity of one to treat the Jews, or the other the Kulaks or Finns, as—to use their own words—vermin.

In the same way, the anti-liberals have sought to wipe out the concept of an impersonal law, built up by slow accretions that reach back into an ancient past, forming a coherent pattern that tends to justice. As in so many other attacks upon liberalism, the fascists have profited by defections within the liberal camp itself. In the United States, for example, it has become a commonplace in "progressive" schools of law during the last generation to hold that all law is judge-made, in the limited sense of the act; and that notions of right and justice, instead of leaving a valid deposit of precedent from generation to generation, are only the fashionable class disguises for the naked fact of power. The mote of observed truth in this doctrine blinds the eye to the essential concept of justice —namely, that which binds the judge.

The fascists, less timid than their "realistic" friends in the liberal camp, carry this attack upon justice to its logical conclusion. They uphold the rule of a minority party or a man; and they preach the absolutism of divine right, as it was called in the seventeenth century, without carrying any of that residual respect which a Louis XIV or a Philip II had for a more ultimate divinity. For these anti-liberals, there is no criterion of justice except the self-interest and the power of the rulers. Thrasymachus said as much in Plato's Republic.

In Nazi Germany and in Fascist Spain the basic concept of law itself has been so completely overthrown that a man may be tried and convicted for a crime that did not exist in law at the time that he committed it. A precious right, obtained by degrees, finally acknowledged by all mature human societies, has been wiped out overnight. Fortunately, there is a simple way to gauge what is best in the liberal tradition. One has only to note those beliefs and practices that fascist systems attack as soon as they get into power. The object of that attack is inevitably something human, precious, essential to man's dignity as man.

It comes to this: the universal elements in liberalism,

the ideal, moralizing elements, are the real focus for fascist aggression. The fascists deliberately muddy the issue by associating freedom with capitalism, as the Nazis attempt to camouflage the object of their aggression by calling the French and English peoples plutocracies. These universal elements arose long before Western capitalism; they were part of the larger human tradition embodied in the folkways of the Jews, in the experimental philosophy of the Greeks, in the secular practices of the Roman Empire, in the sacred doctrines of the Christian Church, in the philosophies of the great post-medieval humanists.

The Marxian notion that ideas are the shadows of the existing economic institutions runs bluntly against facts precisely at this point. For although a culture forms a related organic whole, a residue is left in each period and place which tends to become part of the general heritage of mankind. This residue is small in amount, but infinitely precious. No single race, class, or people can create it or be its keeper. It is like vitamins in the nourishment of the human body: small in quantity, but indispensable for health and growth.

The effort to equate Manchester liberalism with the human traditions of personal responsibility, personal freedom, and personal expression is sometimes shared by the defenders of capitalistic privilege. This is the gross mistake of those who try to tie together private capitalism and "the American way." But these notions are false, whether held by the absolutists of private property, or by the absolutists who would challenge the regime of private property.

Liberalism's most important principles do not belong exclusively to liberalism. Confucius, Socrates, Asoka, Plato, Aristotle testify to them no less than Jefferson and Mill. Liberalism took over this older humanist tradition, revamped it, and finally united it to a new body of hopes and beliefs that grew up likewise in the eighteenth century. This association of the oldest and the newest elements in liberalism has been a source of confusion. Nothing I shall say in the next chapters casts the slightest reflection upon the older form, the form I have called ideal liberalism.

11. HUMANITARIANISM AND POWER

The second element in modern liberalism is that which
has led to its undoing. To many people it seems as important as the first; indeed its modern counterpart. But
in fact this other element in "liberalism" rests upon a
quite different set of premises, both about the nature of
man and the promise of the machine. I shall call it pragmatic liberalism.

Liberalism in the second sense was symbolically a
child of Voltaire and Rousseau: the Voltaire who thought
that the craft of priests was chiefly responsible for the
misery of the world, and the Rousseau who thought that
man was born naturally good and had been corrupted
only by "society" and evil institutions.

This liberalism was, more generally, a by-product of
the inventors and the industrialists of the period who, concentrating upon the means of life, thought sincerely that
the ends of living would more or less take care of themselves. Were not these ends after all simple? The obvious
goal of life for the poor was to become members of the
middle classes, and for the middle classes to enjoy the
luxuries and the privileges of the rich. As for the rich,
their mission was to gather and garner ever larger shares

of the world's goods: the infinite was the measure of their appetites.

This pragmatic liberalism was vastly preoccupied with the machinery of life, as the natural agent of all ideal values: it forgot that engines, no matter how powerful, were in one sense but buckets and shovels dressed up for adults. Characteristically, this creed overemphasized the part played by political and mechanical invention, by abstract scientific thought and practical contrivance. Aware of the very real gains that the sciences had made—above all, in the scientific method itself—this brand of liberalism was unaware of serious losses that had accompanied its progress. Accordingly it minimized the rôle of instinct, tradition, history. It was unaware of the dark forces of the unconscious; it was annoyed by the capricious and the incalculable, for the only universe it could rule was a measured one, and the only type of character it could understand was the utilitarian one. Was not its principal mode of amusement statistics?

The liberal's lack of a sense of history carries a special disability: it makes him identify all his values with the present. Should the present be a shabby one, he quickly comes to the conclusion that the country which exhibits the practical vices and mischiefs he deplores is unworthy of his allegiance. But a country is more than the people and institutions that exist in a single generation. The America we must save today, for example, is not just the

America of shifty politicians and go-getting advertisers and slimy industrialists who would like to "make a deal" with the fascists. Nor is it the America of Hearst, Ford, and Father Coughlin. No self-respecting person would lift a finger to save *that*.

But our America is the America of Adams and Jefferson, the America of Joseph Henry and Audubon and William James, the America of Whitman and Melville and Olmsted and Richardson, the America that may therefore still be realized in time to come by reason of all the ideas and forces and impulses that have come down to us from the past and are pushing into the future. Our country cannot be identified with "capitalism," because many of the most precious parts of our heritage long antedated capitalism and will long survive it.

Abraham Lincoln had about him probably as dismal a lot of peanut politicians, grafters, and plain scoundrels as ever defamed the name of our country before the administrations of Grant and Harding. Saving the American Union was, in effect, saving canny financiers like Jay Cooke, outright rogues like Commodore Vanderbilt, and along with them all the pigs that had got their feet in the trough and were guzzling the swill. If that had been all, the life and blood expended in the Civil War would remain an unbearable mockery.

But what was really saved was infinitely more; nothing less than the continued possibility of a peaceful and honorable life for millions of good honest Americans who were neither get-rich-quicksters nor scoundrels: life for them and life for their children and children's children. And this is why the current contempt for history and tradition is so disastrous: it confines moral and political judgments to a momentary world seen in distorted perspective; whereas the real world has three dimensions in time, and of these the immediate present is by far the least important part.

Those who believe, with pro-fascist Henry Ford, that "History is bunk" are saying in reality that human life is bunk. For the enduring reality of every human community is its history. When history vanishes life itself is at a standstill; condemned to a moment-to-moment existence that has neither direction nor purpose nor the possibility of accumulating significant experience.

The pragmatic liberal thought that science, which asks all questions, would in time also answer them. He was at home in problem-solving situations, and ill at ease in realms like poetry and art and morals, where his type of intellectual technique was an unprofitable one. In order not to be embarrassed by the existence of territory his method did not cover, the pragmatic liberal did not widen his method: he blandly denied the importance of the territory. When this would not work he struggled to limit interest to that narrow portion of reality his method could adequately cover. The evil results of this habit of mind

68

in education are only just beginning to show: they may well contribute to the ultimate downfall of our civilization.

For the pragmatic liberal, only knowledge promoted power; and power, power over other men, power over nature, was the chief goal of knowledge. Without being fully aware of the implications, he sought to attach his humanitarian and ideal sentiments to the sacrificial cult of power: the veritable enemy of what was valid in his philosophy.

The liberal took for granted that the emotional and spiritual needs of man need no other foundation than the rational, utilitarian activities associated with the getting of a living. If these were properly managed, the human personality would adjust itself. In this process of adaptation, the environment, natural or economic or institutional, was supposed to be relatively fixed, or at least obdurate to willful human change. The personality on the other hand was looked upon as essentially plastic, soft, accommodating. Instruments and organizations might, with ampler knowledge, be improved: personalities needed rather to be "adjusted." That there was any inner criterion for this adjustment, that it was no one-way process of passive acquiescence on the part of the self, was a perception which did not fit into the pragmatic scheme.

Because of this overwhelming concern for the external environment as a field of interest, as a center of organized activities, as a subject for scientific description, the prag-

matic liberals lost their early tie with the human personality. Though the scientific exploration of the personality
went farther than it had ever gone in the past, in the great
progress made from Charcot and Janet to Freud and Jung,
the arts of personal development remained on a relatively
primitive level. For pragmatic liberalism avoided the
normative disciplines, those dealing with purposes and
values, rather than abstract matters of fact. Hence a steady
neglect of the fields of esthetics, ethics, and religion, fields
which early modern liberals like Rousseau had duly cultivated. This neglect has gone so far that the books of one
of the most incisive critics of the weakness of liberalism,
Dr. Reinhold Niebuhr, have scarcely been noted for re-
view in "modern" and progressive magazines because their
author happens to be a professor of religion.

In fact, the subjective areas of experience were left
by the liberals to traditional thinkers with the confident
belief that they would eventually drop out of existence,
mere vestiges of the race's childhood. With a few exceptions, the pragmatic liberals have produced no effective
thought in any of these fields since the eighteenth century. As a result of this neglect, many people have been
compelled to live on the debris of past dogmas and buried
formulations. Unconscious, for example, of the sources
of their ethical ideas, these pragmatic liberals pick up
more or less what happens to be lying around them, with-

out any effort at consistency or clarity, still less at effec‹ tiveness: here a scrap left over from childhood, there a fragment of Kant or Bentham, or again a dash of Machia- velli, pacifist Quakers one moment and quaking Nie- tzscheans the next.

12. THE IMMATURITY OF THE MATURE

In short, it is not unfair to say that the pragmatic liberal has taken the world of personality for granted. Without any conscious disavowal, he turned his back in practice upon values, feelings, wishes, purposes, ultimate ends. Like Mr. Gradgrind, in Dickens's "Hard Times," he asked for a definition of horse, and was horrified to find that anyone might have feelings or sentiments that might modify Bitzer's cold definition that it was a gramnivorous quadruped.

The pragmatic liberal assumed either that the world of personality did not exist, or that it was relatively unimportant. At all events, if it did still exist, it could safely be left to itself without cultivation: every man was the best judge of what he liked and felt. Unlike the sixteenth century Protestants who sought individual salvation but assumed that most men were damned, the liberal regarded men as essentially good. Only faulty economic and political institutions kept them from becoming better. These defects were supposed to reside exclusively in the mechanism of society; not in its purposes. That there might be internal obstacles to external improvement seemed to him absurd. And that there was a field for imaginative design and rational discipline in the building of the personality, as much as in the building of a bridge, did not occur to him. A certain self-conceit kept him from suspecting that his own personality might be open to improvement.

Unfortunately for this optimism, we have at long last discovered that immature personalities, irrational personalities, demoralized personalities, are as inevitable as weeds in an untended garden when no deliberate attempt is made to provide a constructive basis for personal development. Craft remained even when priestcraft was abolished. The demonic will-to-power remained, even though the princes were deposed.

Behind this failure to establish, on a fresh basis, a form-giving discipline for the personality was a singular conviction—the belief that it was not needed. Progress, for the pragmatic liberal, consisted in getting away as rapidly as possible from the past: it assumed that mankind's entire experience was a tissue of lies, errors, perversions, stupidities. Now, marvelous though science's discoveries have been, the experience of the race must have precedence over them, when they are temporarily in conflict, until time has given science itself further opportunity to confirm or modify its statements.

In the nineteenth century, for example, the chemists and physiologists discovered the energy values of food. Believing that they had discovered the sole key to effective nourishment, the dietitians of the time published tables to show cheap and simple means of nourishment. Watery foods, such as salads and green vegetables, were discarded except for taste; all the subtle combinations that go into a mixed diet were treated as the fanciful practices of a race that had not yet caught up with science. They might be condoned as trifling pleasures, but they had no place in a scientific diet. In a popular cookbook published forty years ago, carrots were dismissed as mere garnishing.

During the last twenty years however the science of physiology has at last caught up with the knowledge of the race once more. A score of discarded foods have been restored to the diet as absolutely essential to existence; and the diet on which science prided itself fifty years ago has turned out to be in fact a starvation diet, which fortunately people never entirely took over. There are many other departments of life where science, though it may eventually provide more trustworthy knowledge than tradition, can as yet offer no better answer than man's funded stock of knowledge and common sense—or it must remain silent because it has no answer.

By a curious twist of thought, the very people who claimed most loudly that science had no use for norms, believed in blind contradiction that science would eventually provide all the guidance necessary for human conduct. Those who simply "knew how" would also know "why" and "wherefore" and "to what purpose." Did not the advance of science imply an emancipation from an empty institutional religion, from the saws, precepts, moralizings of the past? Such was the innocence of the pragmatic liberal that those who were quite indifferent to ethical standards thought of themselves as "realists." They could hardly understand William James, when he called emotionality the *sine qua non* of moral perception. For their creed ruled out both emotionality and moral perception.

But the fact was that the most old-fashioned theologian, with a sense of human guilt and sin and error, was by far the better realist. Though the theologian's view of the external world might be weak as science, though he might be lazy in combining personal salvation and social aims, he at least knew that the internal world had dimensions of its own. The theologian, like the Ibsens and Tolstoys, understood the world of value and personality; and this included an understanding of those constant human phenomena—sin, corruption, evil—on which the liberal closed his eyes. Not knowing the difference between sin and intellectual error, the liberal might identify stupidity but he had no grasp of sin and evil: for him sin was only a mark of the "mentally immature." In that very conviction he disclosed his own mental immaturity.

PART THREE:

The Undermining of Personality

All err the more dangerously, as they each follow a truth. Their fault is not in following a falsehood, but in not following another truth.

As men are not able to fight against death, misery, and ignorance, they have taken it into their heads, in order to be happy, not to think of them at all.

BLAISE PASCAL

13. THE EVILNESS OF EVIL

"Sin" is an unpopular word, and therefore I have used it deliberately. This word has long dropped out of the vocabulary of educated people; and even those who have remained in the Churches, unless very straitlaced and orthodox, use it—if at all—with a certain feeling of embarrassment, as being a sign that they are old-fashioned and behind the times.

But sin is an indispensable word for describing moral error, errors in conduct, as distinguished from intellectual error, errors in judgment or in practical behavior. The difference is recognized by everyone in practice, even in trivial matters. No one, for example, feels the slightest sense of self-reproach at making a mistake in adding up a column of figures, unless he is a bookkeeper and his professional honor is at stake. One rubs out the error and adds the column up again correctly; that is all. But if one has hastily passed by a person who has fallen on the street without helping him—even if one has the excuse of being late to an important appointment—the feeling of having been found wanting by another human being cannot be rubbed out. It may rankle for days.

The essential difference between these two kinds of error

has been lost sight of in modern society, thanks to the pragmatic liberal's persuasion that only immature minds are open to sin. But the difference is genuine: intellectual error touches only a small segment of one's life; but sin goes much deeper and spreads much wider; it reaches every part of the human frame. Both virtue and sin indeed have this special property of irradiating the personality. Their effects persist long after the occasion has vanished; the train of events they set up may keep on their course even unto the third and the fourth generation.

Sin, likewise, has a certain compensating value; and those who are unconscious of its existence lose this value. For sin, when it is recognized and repented of, frequently enables the sinner to reach a far higher plane of perfection. The recoil of repentance gathers energy for far intenser efforts in the opposite direction. There are plenty of people who live "blameless lives": people who pay their bills, do not quarrel with their neighbors, are reasonably attentive to their wives and families, and go to their grave without leaving behind an enemy or a debt or a tear. Perhaps there are more "blameless people" in the world today than ever before. This is partly because large areas of conduct have been neutralized through knowledge and habit. Dietetics and hygiene have partly removed the necessity for moral invocations against gluttony. (But have they? Or has gluttony in our world only taken more subtle forms?)

At all events, the capacity to sin, or rather the inevitableness of sin, is a constant fact in human experience. Not just an open breaking of rules and laws; but a defiance of that which the sinner himself knows to be best— that is the nature of sin. No one is free from sin. The readiness to sin does not vanish with mental maturity; but rather, on the contrary, every gain in one's powers increases the gravity of one's temptations and the importance of one's moral decisions. Laziness might be a quite venial sin in a ditchdigger. In a General upon whose conduct the life of millions depends, it may become quite literally a mortal sin. Nor can one avoid sin merely by recognizing it, any more than one can avoid influenza because one knows its symptoms. By painstaking attention to one's conduct, however, one may lessen the area of sin and reduce its capacity for damage: this is the effect of all virtuous disciplines. Conduct, as Matthew Arnold put it, is three-fourths of life; and to have no theory of conduct, to have no discipline of conduct, to be unaware that there is a deliberate art of conduct, is to leave the personality itself in a raw, uncultivated state.

The upshot of this argument is simple. Good and evil are real, as virtue and sin are real. Evil is not just a mental aberration, which only pathological characters are the victims of; and sin is not just a symptom of mental immaturity, as the pragmatic liberal would have it. Both these optimistic interpretations of sin and evil lead always

81

to the flattering conclusion that the intelligent cannot sin and that the mentally adult can do no evil. These conclusions are plainly gratifying to those who fancy themselves intelligent and mature, because it leads them to a super-Calvinistic state of grace, in which all things are possible, and whatever one does is blessed.

At that point, the pragmatic liberal and the fascist—coming from opposite poles—meet face to face. And whatever the fascist's contempt for the liberal, there is plenty of evidence at hand to prove that the liberal, face to face with fascism, can literally not find words to condemn it. This refusal to recognize evil as evil has fatally delayed the world's reaction against barbarism.

14. FAILURE TO FACE ULTIMATE ISSUES

Pragmatic liberalism did not believe in a world where the questions of good and evil were not incidental or superfluous, but of radical importance. Its adherents thought they would presently abolish the evils inherent in life by popularizing anesthetics and by extending the blessings of the machine and the ballot.

Such people—they are found in all parties and sects—did not believe in the personal life. They believed in as much of it as could be fitted into practical routine. I recently asked a group of very intelligent educators, men and women well above the average in ability, an informal series of questions to determine what share the cultivation of the inner life had in their calendar of activities. Their honest answers were significant.

How many of them painted or sang or wrote poetry or practiced handicraft for the fun of it or gardened? How many of them read poetry, looked at paintings, listened to music, practiced these arts passively? There were far more in the second group than the first; and perhaps because music is now available through machines, radios and phonographs, there were far more listeners to music than readers of poetry. How many went to church? Perhaps two out of a group of twenty. How many devoted as much as ten minutes a day to pure contemplation—free from all practical demands, empty of any deliberate thought, in short, sustained reverie? None. And note, these were educators, not business men: almost all of them people with eight years of university education behind them.

This is a fairly typical sampling, I believe, of the culture of liberalism. Not merely are the main fields of personality neglected; but in that culture only a small part of the activity that goes on so busily under the labels of art, literature, or religion has the faintest connection with these fields, except in name.

For those who have accepted this bleak world picture, esthetic interests, moral discipline, the habits of contemplation and evaluation, all seem mere spiritual gymnastics. They prefer more physical exercises, which will reduce the girth of the waist or move the bowels. By sheer activity (busy work) the pragmatic liberals keep their eyes manfully on the mere surface of living. This gospel of work, as Carlyle called it, became ingrained in the thought of the nineteenth century. Even Goethe, well-balanced spirit that he was, did not escape it. What is the philosophy of the last part of Faust but the deliberate attempt to shove aside the eternally pressing and the eternally unanswerable problems of knowledge and love by a well-conceived program of public works?

For the sleek progressive mind, the appraisal of death was a neurotic symptom. Happily, science's steady advances in hygiene and medicine might postpone further and further that unpleasant occasion itself. That death has another dimension for man, that man must face death while he lives, to circumvent its mere biological finality, that all his monumental ambitions are in effect ways to surmount death and, so to say, *live it down*—this tragic sense of life was lost in the mere hum and go of the day's work.

Most of the sweetness and decorum of modern society rests on a gentleman's agreement to forget death—death and all its stark anticipations. The slaughter-house, the prison, the hospital, the slum, the asylum, the battlefield, the sewer and the garbage pile and the potter's field all exist and flourish behind this agreement. This is particularly true for the inhabitant of modern urban communities: above all, for the millions who have lost their ties to the old religious cults, rooted in peasant traditions, for whom birth and death are ultimate facts: wonderful and fearful to experience, wonderful and fearful to contemplate.

The pragmatic liberal's failure to confront except in a hurried, shamefaced way the essential facts of life and death has been responsible for much of the slippery thinking on the subject of war that has weakened the moral decision of millions. The present crisis compels democratic peoples to sacrifice everything, even their lives, to preserve their freedom—or to accept servitude, hoping that by shamming dead they may escape notice and avoid actual physical death. One such liberal, in private conversation, told me that he could not make a political decision which might lead to war and thereby bring about the death of other human beings. When I objected that the failure to make such a decision in the existing international situation would certainly lead to the less fruitful death of these same human beings six months or six years hence, he confessed that for him any extra time spared for the private enjoyment of life seemed that much gained.

One need not doubt the honesty of this liberal. But it is obvious that he has ceased to live in a meaningful world. For a meaningful world is one that holds a future that extends beyond the incomplete personal life of the individual; so that a life sacrificed at the right moment is a life well spent, while a life too carefully hoarded, too ignominiously preserved, is a life utterly wasted.

Unless life is conceived as tragedy, in which the ultimate certainty of death counts at every moment in one's actions and plans for living, it becomes little better than a farce. And what a farce! a farce that is funny temporarily only for the fortunate who are not in the spotlight; a farce that becomes a welter of meaningless blows for those that must endure the continued buffetings by grotesque clowns, who use sandbags instead of bladders, and flails instead of slapsticks: a farce too coarse even to provide comedy for the spectator who thinks, too empty to provoke tears in the spectator who feels.

15. FORCE, GRACE, AND REASON

Is it any wonder, then, that the pragmatic liberals in all camps have been incapable of making firm ethical judgments or of implementing them with action? Their color-blindness to moral values is the key to their political weaknesses today. Hence they cannot distinguish between barbarism and civilization.

Worse than this: such color-blindness leads many of these liberals to pass a highly favorable verdict upon barbarism, because of the superior capacity it has shown for reorganizing its economic institutions so that they may serve exclusively for military conquests, putting through public works that gratify the egos of their dictators, and multiplying the engines of war, so that these egos may be further inflated by the tribute exacted from conquered nations. It is more than a sneaking admiration for Nazi barbarism that shows itself in the callous utterances of a Lindbergh—that flattered receiver of Nazi "honors"—or in people like the editors of *Common Sense*.

The latter "liberals" still show more concern over the fact that Huey Long, our first would-be American Fuehrer, was assassinated than over the menace of the movement he started. Indeed their tenderness for the fascists is so acute that they are still aghast over the fact that in "Men Must Act" I called this murder—and now call it again— an extremely fortunate and happy event: one that has averted for the time-being scores of murders, lynchings, brutalities, oppressions upon the part of the gangsters he had gathered around him.

This tenderness toward fascism shows where the hearts of such "liberals" really lie: many of them covertly worship power and cringe before it; they esteem success, and do not concern themselves with the evils sponsored by the successful. One needs no gift of prophecy to see how quickly their liberal coats will turn inside out should fascism ever invade America's shores.

Refusing to recognize the crucial problem of evil, the pragmatic liberals are unable to cope with the intentions of evil men. They look in vain for mere intellectual mistakes to account for the conduct of men who have chosen deliberately to flout man's long efforts to become civilized. In the case of Germany they look to the Treaty of Versailles—itself a work of marvelous magnanimity and high justice, compared with the treaties already inflicted by Stalin and Hitler—for explanations of conduct and ideas that have nothing to do with the first World War or the economic depression that started in 1929.

The fundamental ideology of fascism was first formulated clearly in the sermons, letters, and exhortations of Martin Luther; for Hitler's program today as applied to the world as a whole is little more than Luther's original doctrines, including the fantastic Nazi doctrine of national autarchy, with the top dressing of Christianity removed. (It is characteristic of the general betrayal of liberalism that this doctrine of autarchy has gotten the support in the United States of men like Charles Beard and Stuart Chase.) The raucous hatred that shouts on every page of "Mein Kampf" received its first classic utterance in Luther's denunciation of the Peasants' Rebellion; and the direct line of connection between Luther and Hitler, through Fichte, Nietzsche, and Wagner, is familiar to all those who know the history of German culture.

Since the liberal has sedulously trained himself to look only for the economic and material causes of human events, since he even fancies that there is no other kind, he lacks historic insight into the world that he must deal with. Evil, for him, has no positive dimensions: hence he cannot recognize its long filiations in history, nor its roots in the human personality itself.

The nearest that the pragmatic liberal can get to evil is to conceive it as the mere lack of something whose presence would be good. Poverty is an evil because it indicates the lack of a good, namely riches. For this kind of liberal the most heinous fact about a war is not the evil intentions and purposes that one or both sides may disclose. The evil resides rather in the needless waste of material, the frittering away of energies, the unbearable amount of human suffering, the premature deaths.

These are indeed terrible afflictions: bitter negations of the possibilities of life. But the final evil of war is neither waste nor death; for all energies roll downhill and death happens to all living creatures. Behind all this is a more stubborn kind of evil: the pride and malice of men. In the case of the Nazis, that evil would remain, towering hideously over the landscape, blotting out the very feeblest possibilities of true human living, even if all their conquests were as quick, as "peaceful," as "bloodless" as their rape of the Czech republic. In comparison with that evil, the worst infamy that war can inflict on body and soul is small.

Lacking any true insight into these stubborn facts of human experience—corruption, evil, irrational desire— liberals also fail to understand that evils often lie beyond merely rational treatment. A mere inquiry into causes, however painstaking and objective, or a mere display of reasonableness and good temper in one's own conduct, may not only fail to cure an evil disposition in a sinner but may aggravate it. Unhappily there are times when an attitude of intellectual humility and sympathy are entirely inappropriate to the press of a particular situation. If a neurotic patient is in a dangerously manic state, one may have to put him in a lukewarm bath before one can reduce him to a tractable condition—and one must have force enough to put him there, as well as enough knowledge and self-confidence to act promptly when the emergency arises.

But there are no warm baths one can use for a national psychosis. Unfortunately, too, there may be collective psychoses that resist rational treatment as stubbornly as certain types of insanity. In these cases a malevolent antipathy toward the physician—combined with a contemptuous withdrawal of co-operation—is not only a manifestation of the disease itself but one of the very facts that frustrate a cure. A physician who failed to recognize the existence of such a type and permitted him at large in the community would fail in his duties.

So even if in charity one should recognize the morbid fantasies of the Nazis as the expression of a collective dementia, one's utmost efforts at understanding the source of these neurotic symptoms would not necessarily effect a cure. Normal people are always at the mercy of the maniac's strength and determination unless they have the force as well as the insight to overcome them.

This illustration has wide reference. It applies to all grades of irrational conduct; and it applies, above all, to such conduct when it is accompanied by threats of physical violence, as in fascism's worldwide assault against democracy and civilization today. There are times when active resistance or coercion is the only safeguard against the conduct of men who mean ill against society; and

without doubt, this is one of those times. The alternative
to coercion is not reason; for reason, among civilized
men, must never be absent from the effort at coercion.
The only real alternative to coercion is what the religious
call conversion, salvation, grace, on the part of the offend-
ing person or nation. Such a conversion happened to Paul
of Tarsus on the road to Damascus, when, seeing the light,
he became a follower of Christ instead of the righteous
persecutor of Christians he had been.

Grace, however, is essentially a pre-rational process,
not hostile to reason, but proceeding by a short cut into an
area that reason cannot directly touch. The liberal tends to
minimize the effectiveness of both coercion and conversion,
both force and grace. To admit the existence of these
forces is to lessen somewhat the importance of those rational, scientific, fact-finding, statistical activities in which
he takes such comfort and pride: the only field in which
he is truly at home. But it is hard to point to any large and
significant social change in which all three elements did
not play a part: for life at its brutal barest rests not on
reason but on force. Not accepting this fact, the liberal becomes—like Starbuck in "Moby Dick"—"*morally en-
feebled* by the incompetence of mere unaided virtue or
rightmindedness." (The italics are mine.)

All this is not to belittle the role of reason: far from
it. The neutralized objectivity of the scientific method is
indeed a high contribution not merely to science itself but

to morals. This displacement of limited egoistic wishes, this reference to common data and to objective methods of proof, open to all other competent men, is one of the real contributions of science to the human personality itself: an integral part of the permanent heritage of ideal liberalism. The theologians and the traditional philosophers have hardly appraised this contribution highly enough —though thinkers like A. N. Whitehead are acutely conscious of it.

But reason is not all-important; and it does not work in society through its own unaided convictions. Reason exists in a world in which physical energy and animal vitality, in which emotional reactions and sentiments and deep unconscious drives, contribute at least equal shares to the decision of all issues. The most sublimated personality never escapes connection with that fundament: the flower blooms in proportion to the richness of its soil, to the pungency of the manure that nourishes it. Hence a true history of man cannot confine itself to tracing the growth of reason in human life; nor can a true philosophy assume that reason must some day reign alone and supreme. Force has often defied grace and dethroned reason for centuries; and it may do so again. Even in the best community, force, grace, and reason must flourish together.

16. COERCION AND COMPROMISE

Coercion is, of course, no substitute for intelligent inquiry and no cure in itself for anti-social conduct. But just as there are maladies in the human body which call for surgery rather than diet—though diet, if applied at an early stage, might have been sufficient—so there are moments of crisis in society when anti-social groups or nations that resist the ordinary methods of persuasion and compromise must be dealt with by coercion.

In such moments, to hesitate, to temporize, only gives the disease a deeper hold upon the organism. And to center one's efforts upon changing the mind of one's opponent, by opposing reason to his irrationality, and to overlook the elementary precaution of depriving him of his weapons for attacking one, is to commit a fatal offense against the very methods one seeks to uphold.

The issue of slavery in the United States is a case in point. I use it because it closely parallels the present issue of the spread of fascism, and yet is far enough away to be seen in perspective. Not merely that, but one may hope at this day and distance that a sympathetic understanding of the South's point of view need not enfeeble one's resistance to contemporary barbarism.

Now in perspective, the great facts in that issue were these: the best spirits in the South, certainly its greatest leader, Robert E. Lee, a soldier who had many of the attributes of a saint, were deeply opposed to the institution of slavery. By the same token, some of the foulest forces in the North, centered in the venal commercialism of New York, were in hearty sympathy with the cause of slavery: witness creatures like Fernando Wood. Even abolitionists like Garrison, in a panic of righteous pacifism, were ready to surrender every moral principle at stake and let the South slip out of the Union in order to avoid the ultimate decision by war.

For twenty-five years the controversy between the two sides had mounted. To Calhoun's original plea for secession was added another demand: the right to maintain slavery and widen its dominions. First autarchy: then conquest. This follows very closely the present fascist pattern, which originally proposed merely to secede from European co-operations and then speedily widened its own field of exploitation, first in Abyssinia and Spain, now throughout the world.

No mere prolongation of the controversy, in the face of the South's resistance to reason and its threats of domination, could have brought about a peaceful solution. Lincoln's offers of appeasement parallel Chamberlain's and proved as ineffective. His policy was shattered because of the new planter class's deliberate intention to maintain and perpetuate its form of barbarism: human slavery. To have effected a resolution of this issue without force something more than a rational method for buying up the slaves and pensioning off the institution was required: nothing less than an act of grace, similar to that which the Russian aristocracy showed itself capable of during this very period, when it abolished the institution of serfdom.

People sometimes assume that slavery would have been wiped out on this continent anyway in the course of time, without warfare, even if the South had achieved independence. They assume that such institutions vanish merely because they are, from a narrow commercial point of view, uneconomical. But those who take this position unconsciously rely upon the nineteenth century shibboleth of progress. For them the prolongation of slavery, still more its spread, is simply "unthinkable."

Before 1925 one might perhaps have defended that ingenuous view; in which case the War between the States was an entirely senseless one, which skillful statesmanship could have averted: the mere result of abolitionist propaganda and hot-headed sentiment. But such a reading of events is now extremely naive. Slavery, which had few passionate defenders even in the South before 1800, had many defenders even in the North by 1860. Hence one must now interpret the development of slavery in the United States, not as a mere survival, but as a fresh jump into barbarism. Slavery, then, was "modern," as fascism prides itself on being today.

In other words, we can now see that slavery was a fore-runner of the grosser forms of barbarism and more universal codes of servility that the fascist states seek to perpetuate today: just as the political boss, with his gangster armies in American cities, is a crude prototype of the Fuehrer's and Duce's who now strut on the international stage, because what was originally only a small local spot of decay now threatens to cover the surface of the planet. (The political boss lacked wider power because he had not the wit or the tradition that would make Bossism a religion. He was content with easy pickings—limited objectives.)

But for the active use of overwhelming physical force, the institution of slavery might have gotten a permanent grip over the whole American continent. He who still believes otherwise has no insight into modern history.

That force alone is not sufficient to settle such critical issues with finality the mental attitude of the South since the War between the States definitely shows. For though force could keep this new weed from spreading, only grace could have uprooted it from the hearts of the defeated Southerners: such a grace as might have spontaneously filled men's hearts in both South and North if the generous intentions of Lincoln, if the noble understanding of Melville and Whitman, could have been carried into the relations between the two parts of the country. That grace was needed on *both* sides.

For the Southern critics were right: industrialism had polluted the North, with degradations to the human soul quite as real and quite as serious as those that slavery had imposed. The free labor of the North obeyed the lash of starvation; and the self-righteousness of the industrialists and financiers of the North over the outcome of the war stank to heaven. Only the saving sense that the North, too, had sinned, that every Northerner still had equivalent evils to redeem, in the slums of New York and Fall River and Pittsburgh—indeed wherever the raw energies of industrialism had penetrated—only this saving sense of guilt could have promoted a similar unbending of the proud Southern neck.

The South rightly resented the North's pretense of indisputable moral superiority; a superiority which masked the cold methodical clutch of Northern business: fat profits that went hand in hand with an unctuous morality.

The mischiefs and miseries of the post-Civil War period in the United States rose essentially out of the absence of grace on both sides; and this in turn was partly due to the fact that a working consciousness of the profound truth of the doctrine of original sin had vanished. The essence of that doctrine is that all men are sinners, the righteous no less than the wicked—and the righteous most of all as soon as they forget that fact.

The too common notion that evil must not be combated by any other means than intellectual understanding and practical adjustments follows from the failure to understand the role that force and grace must always play. Always, the liberal's humanitarian impulses make him afraid that those who attempt to combat evil may ultimately have to use physical force—which is as though a doctor should be afraid of treating a patient because if his regimen is unsuccessful he may have to operate on him with the knife. Guarding his virtue, the liberal refuses to become soiled in the act of fighting: blindly he prefers to suffer the much more serious stain of submitting to injustice. This is a gospel of despair. But the fact that it is common perhaps explains the liberal's defeatist response to fascism during the last decade. So afraid is he of practicing violence himself that he surrenders in advance whilst he still possesses adequate weapons.

In practice, this moral finicking means turning the world over to the rule of the violent, the brutal, and the inhuman, who have no such fine scruples, because the humane are too dainty in their virtue to submit to any possible assault on it: for them, self-pollution is as hideous as rape and murder put together. So in the tolerant attempt to give the devil his due, liberalism meets barbarism halfway, in a mood of complaisance, if not of fawning acquiescence; and on the theory that war is the worst of evils, the liberals have tearfully acquiesced in

100

the rule of those who, as Blake said, "would forever depress mental and prolong corporeal war."

Now the dangers of active resistance to evil are real. Only mummies are ever safe from the mischance of life. Force *does* coarsen the users of it, no matter how virtuous their purposes. When blood is spilt, anger *does* rise and reason temporarily disappears. In men of good will these lapses are temporary; in the course of time their moral balance returns, as it returned steadily to the British and the French from 1924 onward, and made it possible for them to rectify, long before Hitler climbed to power, most of the major blunders and sins committed at the end of the first World War.

Force, therefore, is not to be used daily in the body politic, like food or exercise. It is only to be used in an emergency, like medicine or the surgeon's knife. Fascism's violation of human standards does not come from the fact that it uses force, but arises from its preferring force to rational accommodation. Fascism deliberately turns mental and physical coercion into human nature's daily food. Under such a regime, coercion permanently displaces grace and reason: war becomes in effect the ruling mode of life, and violence, with all its barbaric excitements, becomes the chief end of the dominant class—or the master nation.

But those who think that fascism can be met by appeasement or reasonable compromise or by "adjustment"

—that word which conceals so much cowardice—surrender their cause in advance. People who pride themselves on their "realism" here are actually betraying their fatal incapacity to understand the evils they confront. Such people pursue an illusory perfection and achieve an actual paralysis. Force cannot be left behind, no matter how humane and rational one's standards of conduct. He who under no circumstances and for no human purposes will resort to force abandons the possibility of justice and freedom.

Mahatma Gandhi has seen this fact clearly; and the war without violence that he preaches is still war: it openly sacrifices the lives of his followers in order to achieve their purposes. It is precisely this readiness to die through passive resistance that has given Gandhi's movement its real successes. Gandhi knows that justice cannot be purchased as cheaply as the timid and the cowardly would desire—by words alone. Words are blanks until they are joined to deeds; and deeds are empty till they are connected with a life and a chain of lives.

Gandhi's method has worked admirably in India, for the British, despite their anomalous position as empire-builders, believe in freedom and have given it to the peoples they have conquered. Even when they have delayed to do so, as in India, they have themselves begotten and fomented the idea, and spread it among the Hindus, who had for so long slumbered in pacific resignation under their own Mogul despots. Gandhi's opponents, moreover, are normal human beings, and there is still more than a vestige of Christian culture in the makeup of the most insensitive British commander: hence outrages like that at Amritsar, which killed and wounded a few hundred people at most, awakened protest from one end of the Empire to the other; whereas outrages of similar nature that now involve, not a few hundred but millions of human beings, who come under Hitler's unscrupulous attacks, leave the world as silent as it is helpless.

Against a foe like the fascist Yahoos, who mow down defenseless refugees *on principle,* in order to demoralize their nation, Gandhi's passive resistance, his war of peaceful sacrifice, would be altogether in vain. Fascism has opened up new depths of depravity which even Gandhi's gallant method cannot touch. The open exultation of Mussolini's son over the terror he provoked when he dropped bombs on a defenseless Abyssinian village is a measure of the evils we must now deal with.

One-sided pacifism, then, leads only to abject surrender and humiliation. For power, defiant of moral checks, destitute of human values, bows only to a greater power. The German socialists took their legalistic pacifism seriously; they got their reward in the concentration camp. The English laborites, following the nerveless Tory leadership, took the same position in international affairs; and that led not alone to the betrayal of the Czech Repub-

lic but to the present endangerment of Western civilization as a whole. A worldwide holocaust has taken place
because the courage to exert force, with rational purpose,
on behalf of a moral principle, was lacking in the statesmen and parties in power in the Western democracies.
This includes our own country, for Mr. Roosevelt's betrayal of the Spanish Republic may prove the most critical mistake of his entire administration.

Despite these sinister examples, the same guileless reasoning has driven many of our American liberals into a
similar position of queasy non-resistance, on the ground
that the only motive that could sanction our opposition to
Hitlerism would be our belief that those who opposed
him, including ourselves, were spotless. These people
say that those who have not clean hands must not use
them at all. The logic is as sound as it would be to say
that a policeman who has committed adultery may not,
in the performance of his duty, arrest a murderer.

People who think of issues in these terms are secretly
complimenting themselves on virtues that neither themselves nor their country possesses; they are guilty of that
most typical sin of the intellectual, the sin of Phariseeism.
Rather, it is because we, too, are not without guilt that
we may oppose fascism with a clean heart. Virtue like dirt
shows quantitative differences: there is a difference between the normal dirt that must be swept out of the house
each morning, and the mud and ordure that accumulates

in a pigsty. Those who cannot see any difference between the sins of the British Empire and the sins of Nazi Germany are incapable of making this elementary quantitative distinction.

In every situation, the relative weight that must be given to coercion or to rational persuasian hinges upon the time that is available for effecting the necessary social change. The shorter the time and the more unprepared a community for action, the less can persuasion be relied upon and the more coercion must be brought into play. If one has only a year to change habits that would require half a generation to alter by education the more forceful must be the methods that are used.

The faceless ones, by murderous application of force and terrorism, have been able to work unbelievable changes in the established mode of life in fascist countries within a few short years. This lesson must not be unheeded by democracy. If democracy is to preserve its very existence, the majority must not scruple to use any necessary amount of coercion upon minority groups who might, if the danger were less, be converted by the slow process of reason, or blandly ignored. To give fascism all the quick benefits of coercion and to hold for democracy all the disabilities of persuasion is to commit suicide.

Unlike fascism, democracy has no need or reason to prolong the present crisis; and once fascism is smashed, democracy will be able to restore the more leisurely, complicated methods of rational persuasion. But to sacrifice the very existence of democracy to the rational principle of persuasion is itself a high irrational act: it is on the same plane of pseudo-morality and crazy ethical absolutism as the effort of the National Civil Liberties Union to preserve free speech and assemblage for fascism's agents and abettors.

Fortunately, our American democracy has a far saner example of the limits of toleration in the conduct of Abraham Lincoln during the Civil War. He did not hesitate even to suspend the writ of Habeas Corpus, far more ancient than our Bill of Rights, when the actions of traitors and copperheads made such a move imperative. For neither our constitution nor our Bill of Rights nor our American traditions would survive, if the nation itself went under: democracy must at least have the resolution to ensure its own survival.

This is why the minimum precautions necessary for fighting fascism *as long as fascism remains in existence* must include keeping every fascist group or pro-fascist speaker off the air, denying the use of the United States mails to every fascist publication—likewise to fascist governments seeking to spread their propaganda; submitting to a National Board of Censorship every item given out by the governments of Germany, Italy, Russia, or Japan, or any of their fascist allies; and finally putting into jail—or sending into exile—the active ringleaders of fascism, under a law which would make the espousal of fascism itself an act of treason against democracy.

To be too virtuous to live is the characteristic moral perversion of liberalism in our generation. Critical of traditional religious precepts, the pragmatic liberal unconsciously sticks to a moral absolutism that no religion could have maintained without wiping out either itself or its part of the human race. Traditional Christianity, for example, believes in virginity as the highest state of the soul. But one of the great sacraments of the Christian Church is marriage, with its carnal obligations. If this common sense had not prevailed, the world would have been depopulated of Christians. Misplaced virtue, indeed, is not the least of human vices. Every virtue has its fitting time and place, and the liberal who grants complete freedom of speech and assembly to the parties that have vowed to exterminate freedom of speech and assembly, along with every other democratic institution, has as little reason to pride himself as the young man who defends his purity, in the fashion of Joseph Andrews, on his marriage night. The time and the place and the press of reality call for a different attitude.

While the liberal fatuously "suspends judgment" on the acts of the fascists, those acts continue to spread torture and infamy, malice and lies, misery and slavery, throughout the world. Such purity leaves behind a foul odor, as of something that has long been dead.

17. THE DREAD OF THE EMOTIONS

The essential moral weakness of liberalism is coupled with a larger weakness in its philosophy. Along with the pragmatic liberal's admirable respect for scientific study and experimental practice goes an over-valuation of intellectual activities as such, and an under-rating of the emotional and feeling sides of life. In the liberal theology, emotions have taken the place of a personal devil.

Now, as every good psychologist knows, and as Count Korzybski has ably demonstrated, emotions and feelings associated with the most remote body-processes are involved in all thought. Behind every symbol we use rationally stands, if one examines it closely, the whole human personality. It is only the intellectually half-baked who think that the meaning of a proposition can be described in terms of a simple connection between the words used and the things referred to. On the contrary, to modify that meaning and give it a closer correspondence to reality is the experience of the person using the word: that and all the inherited usages of his community.

The difficulty and the magic of communication are centered on this very spot. Without these personal and social contexts, sharable only by those who have had similar experiences, words are just empty sounds. Behind speech is the unspeakable; and the emotions are a constant part of that unspeakable matrix of experience.

Reason and emotion, then, have the same common root: the personality and the community as a whole, with its past and future, too, as well as its narrower present. Their detachment from this deep inaccessible soil, their division into the separate realms of science and art, are purely practical devices of limited use. It is always the distinction of great art in every age that it is close to the leading philosophical and scientific ideas of that age: this is what makes a Dante, a Leonardo, a Goethe, a Whitman so immensely more important than their lesser contemporaries; and it is the only valid connection between the work of a Shakespeare and a Bacon. This argument holds in reverse, too: for on the heights of science, among people like Pascal, Leibniz, Newton, Faraday, Clerk-Maxwell, Geddes, and Einstein, is a degree of emotional awareness that records itself in their continued interest in man's most profound emotional expressions, above all, in religion.

Thought about political and social situations that is empty of emotion and feeling, that bears no organic relation to life, is just as foreign to effective reason as emotion that is out of proportion to its stimulus or without rational contexts. The body, the unconscious, the prerational, are all important to sound thought. To imagine that the mind works better when it is cut off from this soil is to imagine that a paper rose possesses of itself a finer odor than a real one.

But because the pragmatic liberal has sought no positive discipline for emotion and feeling, there is an open breach between his affective life and his intellectual interests. He distrusts the first; he pays little attention to it; he narrows its place in his personal life; and when he starts to think, he seeks—supposedly in the interests of objectivity—to dispense with it altogether. His first impulse in any situation is to get rid of his emotions because they may cause him to go wrong. He sees no alternative between frigidity and panic.

Unfortunately for this effort to achieve clarity by forming a purely intellectual judgment on the basis of facts, the liberal is forced to disregard one of the most important points in any social situation, namely, that it arouses certain feelings, sentiments, and emotions, which inherently belong to that situation. To overlook this fact is a monstrous and willful piece of subjectivity; and it is a far more serious source of scientific inaccuracy than the emotions themselves.

In short, intellectual judgment, eviscerated of all emotional references and labeled "realistic," is the prime source of the pragmatic liberal's errors in dealing with the conduct of his fellow men. In his very effort to become impartial, he exercises a curiously perverted kind of partiality—that of renouncing a large part of the human personality. This gives him a feeling of godlike unruffledness at the very moment he is making an ass of himself.

This error was shockingly exemplified in the pronouncement signed in the spring of 1940 by four hundred American scientists who begged the President to keep America out of war. Their reason was a highly original one: they had made the surprising discovery that war destroys the values of civilization. That the deliberate extermination of objective intellectual research throughout the world might follow the worldwide victory of the fascists did not, apparently, occur to the minds of these imperturbable scientists. Like Archimedes, these people will be surprised in their bathtubs when the Nazi legionaries trample in. And if they are slaughtered or imprisoned, who can say that they have not brought that fate upon themselves? When the barbarians are loose, Archimedes should not be caught in the bathtub, nor should he be caught solemnly praying for a peace that will be granted only through the barbarian's death-dealing victory, if no active steps are taken to prevent it.

The deliberate attempt to castrate the emotions is precisely what has caused the liberal mind to go wrong in facing the foul realities of the present world. The calmness and sang-froid of Benes were perhaps his most serious weakness during the long period before the Munich crisis:

111

ominously he repeated the self-defeating mood of Bruening in the days before his removal. The mediocre emotional responses of a Chamberlain or a Daladier were not
the smallest handicaps to their fumbling statesmanship: in
fact, they probably contributed as much to the debacle as
the maniacal hyperactivity of Hitler.

Plainly, it is the people who have remained calm, assured, unmoved, in the present crisis who have given all
the breaks to their opponents. Just before Gamelin's fall
an article appeared in which his imperturbable calmness
and good digestion were praised. Fatal defects! The
French army might have been able to meet the German
onslaught better had Gamelin died of emotional hyperten-
sion and physical overstrain in the eight months of grace
that were given him.

Instead of priding himself on not being carried away
by his emotions the liberal should rather be a little
alarmed because, for lack of exercise, he often has no
emotions that could under any circumstances carry him
away.

This is not a new criticism. Graham Wallas lectured on
the subject twenty years ago. He showed that in all valid
thinking which referred to human situations it was important to be able to use the emotions, not to put them
into cold storage. Pragmatic liberalism, by and large, has
prided itself upon its colorlessness and its emotional neutrality; it has in fact regarded these qualities as the very

hallmark of objectivity. This suspicion of passion is partly responsible for the liberal's ineptitude for action. In a friendly world, pragmatic liberalism leads to nothing worse than a tepid and boring life; but in a hostile world it may easily lead to death.

Let me give, in conclusion, a simple illustration. If one meets a poisonous snake on one's path, two things are important for a *rational* reaction. One is to identify it, and not make the error of assuming that a copperhead is a harmless adder. The other is to have a prompt emotion of fear, if the snake *is* poisonous; for fear starts the flow of adrenin into the blood-stream, and that will not merely put the organism as a whole on the alert, but it will give it the extra strength needed either to run away or to attack. Merely to look at the snake abstractedly, without identifying it and without sensing danger and experiencing fear, may lead to the highly irrational step of permitting the snake to draw near without one's being on guard against his bite.

The lack of a sense of danger in the presence of fascism, which has alas! characterized both the parties of the right and the left in all the democracies, is in no little part accountable for their utter unpreparedness to cope with that danger. The people who responded to the danger signals were dismissed as hysterical. Because the pragmatic liberal persistently believes that his own country's emotions will be uncontrollable, he lets himself submit to other countries where no effort whatever is made to control the emotions. But why do emotions to the arid liberal mean "panic" or "hysteria"? The answer is simple: being entirely unused to the life of the emotions, he is unaware of the means by which better balanced personalities *utilize* them and control them.

That is why the instincts of simpler people in the present crisis have been sounder than the instincts of intellectuals. I find I can trust my country neighbors, farmers, housepainters, garagemen, grocers, to be more intelligent about the need for drastic action than most metropolitan intellectuals with half a dozen years more of formal education. My neighbors are not subtle enough to be as stupid as a George Soule or a John Haynes Holmes: they still know enough to draw their hand away from a hot fire; and they still have enough human decency to stop their work or break off their dinner to help a neighbor whose place is threatened by a grass fire. Their emotions are still on tap; and in that sense they are far better men and women than those who pretend to lead them and give them advice.

Pragmatic liberalism, under the assumption that men ideally should think without emotion or feeling, deprives itself of the capacity to be human. This is one of the gravest features of the present crisis: the cold withdrawal of human feeling by large masses of people today is almost as terrible a crime against civilization as the more malignant inhumanity of the fascists. Under the guise of preserving their sanity, the tolerant and the neutral freeze into indifference. And they justify their withdrawal by despicably dwelling on old wrongs—as a neighbor might refuse to rescue the family next door, despite the fact that his own house might soon catch fire, because the head of that family had borrowed ten dollars and never returned it.

18. THE CURSE OF OPTIMISM

Closely allied with the liberal's emotional anesthesia is his incurable optimism. This is a wrinkled smile left over from the eighteenth century when, in the first flush of confidence, the possibilities of human advance seemed boundless.

Now this optimism belonged originally to a constructive and expanding age. In its inception, it was a healthy reaction against the moldering institutions and precedents of the past. But it has become an unfortunate handicap in the present period; for now the destructive forces are gaining the upper hand, and, in the approaching stabilization of population and industry, the malevolence of the human will on the part of the propertied classes may—as already in Germany and Italy—give unlimited power to those who represent barbarism.

To apply to this age of hardship, danger, and difficulty the complacent, sanguine attitudes of the eighteenth century is to be unarmed for the active emergencies we must meet.

Now destruction, malice, violence hold no temptation for the liberal or for the vast body of people who bask unthinkingly in this philosophy, even though they may be formally connected with the tougher view of the historic religions. In the kindness of his heart, the liberal cannot bring himself to believe that these evils can seriously influence the conduct of any large part of mankind. Are not all men rational, or at least well-meaning? Do they not all want tangible rewards, like three square meals and a social security check when they are out of work?

The liberal cannot understand the irrational element in fascism, which gives it its driving force and its vast powers for destruction. He could not understand any better than Chamberlain that the gift of the Czech Republic to Hitler could not appease him; but was rather an insult that needed to be avenged. One might as well offer the carcass of a dead deer in a butcher store to a hunter who values it only as a symbol of his personal prowess in hunting. And that is why all talk of economic adjustments and understandings with the fascist states, which would enable them to live at peace with their neighbors, is muddled nonsense. It is not possible now and it was not possible half a dozen years ago. For this notion assumes the continuation of the liberal's utilitarian and humanitarian world; and it is that which the fascist rejects.

For the fascist the tearing down of the fabric of modern civilization is not an incident in achieving his economic ambitions: *it is a career in itself, the center of his hopes, his beliefs, his desires.* Unfortunately, it is not in Ricardo or Marx or Lenin, but in Dante and Shakespeare and

117

Dostoyevsky that an understanding of the true sources of fascism are to be found. Those sources are in the human soul, not in economics. The same economic milieu that produced Joan of Arc placed at her side the incredibly cruel and infamous Gilles de Rais. Overweening pride, delight in cruelty, neurotic disintegration—in this and not in the Treaty of Versailles or the incompetence of the German Republic lies the explanation of fascism. In neurotic disturbances the disease itself may become a center of integration and supply the emotional sources for a career.

The over-simple economic explanation of human motives fails because of a fact well known in human psychology: the same stimulus may cause different responses, or different stimuli may cause the same response. Given any particular economic situation, there is almost always more than one way of meeting it. If one is out of work and without food one may die meekly of starvation; or one may beg in the streets; or one may borrow money from a neighbor—or rob a grocery store. Each action is a response to the same situation; and in each case the result is the same, food. The personal choice however is not completely free or unconditioned: it is such a choice as appears valid to the chooser, in the light of his experience and purpose; and it is such a choice as is actually left open by the situation. Plainly, the economic need cannot be divorced from the historic and the ethical moment.

Economic explanations of social disorder reflected a

118

genuine reality in the nineteenth century. But why? Because the industrial world itself had captured men's fancies and excited their dreams. But these same explanations disguise a reality in a day of economic disillusionment: the reality of the barbaric will-to-power, the claim to conquest and booty. There are no limits to that claim: it is totalitarian by nature and it wants the whole earth. Nothing can stop it except the capacity of free peoples to resist it.

Unfortunately, what is going on in Asia and Europe today, what may be going on in America presently unless the present popular revulsion of feeling transforms itself rapidly into effective action, is going on with the liberal's permission. For his philosophy is helpless to understand the nature of the evil and the irrational, or to take any steps to resist the merciless aggression that springs from them.

The incurable tendency of the liberal is to believe the best about everybody. That is the defect of a great quality, the sense of good will and comity that did indeed grow up in the nineteenth century: a truly civilizing attitude. Unfortunately, the existence of fascism makes this virtue impossible; indeed its continued practice in a community haunted by the aggressions of fascism is almost as much a treasonable act as the attempt to preserve the free speech of fascists and their open allies.

In the evacuation of the British and French armies from

Flanders an innocent-looking civilian approached a company of French soldiers waiting for their boat. Instead of challenging him, the soldiers let him come close; whereupon he threw wide his cape and opened up a murderous machine gun fire that killed off most of them. It is precisely because the fascists count upon this elemental faith in human decency to serve their maniacal purposes that they have been so successful. After using parachute troopers disguised as monks, civilians, or soldiers dressed in uniforms of their enemies, in defiance of long-honored rules of warfare, the Germans could nevertheless count upon American newspapers to be gullible enough or humorless enough to print their denunciation of the shooting of parachutists while in the air: denunciations by that Goering whose "word of honor" as a Prussian officer still obscenely mocks its many victims.

It is a vice, then, in times like the present to hope when there is no reason to hope and to exhibit the nicest moral qualms, the most delicate intellectual scruples, in situations that demand that one wade in coarsely and exert one's utmost efforts.

All the slippery optimism which has so devitalized the democratic peoples has sprung, not from accidental misjudgments about particular events; it has sprung from an essential defect, which is best seen, in its intellectual nakedness, in the philosophy of pragmatic liberalism. We now face a world that is on the brink, perhaps, of another Dark Age. And because a Dark Age is not included in the liberal chronology, the liberal glibly refuses to accept the evidence of his senses. Like the sundial, he cannot tell time on a stormy day.

19. THE BETRAYAL OF LIBERALISM

Now one must remember that liberalism has two sides. There is an ideal liberalism, deeply rooted in the example and experience of humanity: a doctrine that commands the allegiance of all well-disposed people. To preserve that inheritance is one of the first duties of man. Without it, the ape and the hyena in human form will roam through our cities.

On top of this, there is a transient doctrine, that of pragmatic liberalism, which grew up in the eighteenth century out of a rather adolescent pride in the scientific conquest of nature. This is the side that concentrates upon purely intellectual issues, that worships the outer power of machines and denies the inner powers of men.

What is important in ideal liberalism are elements like the great Roman conception of humanity, united in the pursuit of freedom and justice, embracing all races and conditions. This is a permanent human bequest. Such an ideal is radically opposed at every point to fascist autarchy. And again, this ideal is no less opposed to the isolationism, moral and political and physical, so long advocated by a large wing of American liberals, including of course their reactionary allies. What is this, in fact, except a passive, milk-and-water version of the fascist's contemptuous attitude toward the rest of the human race?

Plainly, the liberal who proposes to do nothing on behalf of the rest of humanity until the lives of his own countrymen are threatened will have very little left to save. The enslaved nations of Europe, who refused to ally themselves with their neighbors and thought they individually could escape, have learned this by now. Too late! For life is not worth fighting for: bare life is worthless. Justice is worth fighting for, order is worth fighting for, culture— the co-operation and communion of the peoples of the world—is worth fighting for. These universal principles and values give purpose and direction to human life.

At present the liberals are so completely deflated and debunked, they have unconsciously swallowed so many of the systematic lies and beliefs of barbarism, that they lack the will to struggle for the essential principles of ideal liberalism, justice, freedom, truth. The only thing that will remove their isolationism is the possible triumph of the fascists over the British. At that moment, it is easy to foresee, these isolationists will become enthusiastically in favor of intercourse in every possible way, and collaboration on any possible terms, *with the fascists:* they will be as fulsome in praise of that black and bastard internationalism as Senator Robert Reynolds—or Lindbergh —or an avowed fascist like Lawrence Dennis.

What is the final result? Pragmatic liberalism has flatly

betrayed ideal liberalism; and if given the chance will betray it further. The values that belong to the latter have been compromised away, vitiated, ruthlessly cast overboard. The permanent heritage of liberalism has been bartered for the essentially ignoble notion of national security, though that, in two short months, has been proved a grotesque illusion. These pragmatic liberals, even now, are loath to conceive the present war as one waged by fascist barbarism against civilization and democracy. Many hold fast to the notion, as a sick baby might cling to a rubber nipple, that the present war is just an old-fashioned contest of power between two imperialist systems, and that the world will be no different no matter which state is triumphant. These liberals dislike anyone to use the word "barbarism" in this instance, because they say—reaching for a brochure from the Institute for Propaganda Analysis—that the use of such words is the fallacy of "calling names."

But it was not the English who first applied the word "Hun" to the Germans: it was the German Kaiser. So it is not people like the present writer who alone call the fascists barbarians, and accuse them of deliberately attacking civilization. It is the leading representatives of fascist thought and fascist government, who have proclaimed this. It is Spengler, the German philosopher of history, who exulted in the fact that the new type of man was once more a beast of prey; it was Ludendorff and Rosenberg who urged the repatriation of the tribal gods of Germany; it was Hitler who proclaimed openly in "Mein Kampf" his purpose to use limitless lies and false promises to confuse his enemies and encompass their defeat. By conveniently forgetting facts of this order, the liberal preserves an air of sanctimonious tolerance—and reproaches those who use a more exact terminology, under which barbarism is called barbarism and bestiality is called bestiality.

Though many of our liberals were moved by the plight of the Spanish republicans, they have long since managed to insulate themselves from any human feeling over the fate of the bullied Czechs, the tortured Jews, the murdered Poles, the basely threatened Finns, the cowed Netherlanders, the humiliated French—or the British who may in fact be exterminated before this book drops off the press. This same beautiful equipoise they have maintained, no less impassively, in turning away from the horrors that have befallen the Chinese. Their very sense of human brotherhood is gone. They have eyes and see not; they have ears and hear not; and in their deliberate withholding of themselves from the plight of humanity they have even betrayed their own narrow values; for they are now witnessing the dissolution of those worldwide co-operations upon which the growth of science, technics, and industrial wealth depends.

This corruption has bitten deep into pragmatic liberalism; even as it has vitiated the conduct of many who profess to be orthodox Christians.

No doubt American liberals have meant well and will continue to mean well; but the fatal sin of the intellectual is the failure to use his mind competently and honestly. In some liberals there will be a belated deathbed repentance. Still others, with the unction of a Chadband, a Pecksniff, or a Uriah Heep, will in the very moment they alter their attitudes seek to make it appear that they never for a moment felt or thought otherwise. But they have all clung, far too long, to the illusion that they could save themselves and their country by cutting themselves off—to use Hawthorne's words in "Ethan Brand"—from the magnetic chain of humanity. Too late they may discover that they are indeed cut off: they can no longer aid humanity, and humanity, in *their* hour of need, can no longer aid them.

PART FOUR:

Crumbled Traditions

Our culture must therefore not omit the
arming of the man. Let him hear in season
that he is born into the state of war, and
that the commonwealth and his own well-
being require that he should not go dancing
in the weeds of peace.

RALPH WALDO EMERSON

20. SOURCES OF TRADITION

Many of the beliefs and attitudes that I have been examining are now so widespread that they do not belong to any philosophical group or political party. One can trace them back to pragmatic liberalism; but they have spread so far from their source that many people have absorbed them, as they breathe the air, without the faintest consciousness of their historic connections. This pragmatic liberalism has, without doubt, been the dominant mode of belief for the last century and a half, and in educated circles for even longer.

Many people who think of themselves as upholders of tradition are really upholding only the meager tradition of pragmatic liberalism. Some who reject "liberal" or "progressive" ideas in politics, accept them in morals. Pragmatic liberalism is the main ingredient of the Western mind: particularly in the realm of politics and business. Always and everywhere, the practical and pragmatic sides outweigh the ideal side.

The decay and partial rebirth of traditionalism is one of the outstanding facts of the last century and a half. Partly this is due to the fact that traditionalists, being allied to the past, lost their hold on a world that was undergoing rapid technological and political changes. Traditional beliefs fought a sort of stubborn rear-guard movement against the advance of science and against the rising belief that the conquest of nature was more important than the salvation of the souls of individual men.

But the decay of traditionalism actually set in long before modern industrialism got under way: it coincided with the growth of the cult of power; and it is hard to say whether the falling away of orthodox religious beliefs was accountable for the onset of capitalism and the expansion of militarism or whether the rise of these institutions progressively hemmed in the activities that were once performed by the two great mainstays of tradition: the home and the Church.

As with liberalism, one is forced to lump together in the traditional group a complex mixture of institutions and beliefs: one must include the Calvinists no less than the Catholics, and Hindus no less than Christians. One must include all those national and regional movements which had their foundations in a return to the past, and the recovery of a local tradition that had often been wiped out by foreign rulers and despots. Traditional, highly traditional, was the re-awakening of national literary currents in the nineteenth century. The sense that the language of a people was a precious bond, that it was their peculiar treasure and creation, the outward symbol of their inner vitality, was one of the most conservative perceptions of the nineteenth century.

Soon after local languages and dialects, local ballads and stories, began to drop out of existence, there arose a new race of scholars and patriots who restored these lost traditions. The recovery of Gaelic in Ireland, the exhumation of Hebrew by the Jews, are prime examples of traditionalism. At the moment when every educated Russian spoke French, and held that Western institutions were destined to civilize Russia from its shaggy barbarism, Dostoyevsky joined the Slavophils, and young social revolutionaries discovered the social virtues of the mir and the artel: primitive forms of peasant and handicraft co-operatives.

One may group together, as distinct from pragmatic liberalism, all the various threads and strands of traditionalism that have survived into the twentieth century. But one must remember that the distinction is only a rough one; and that there is a large transitional area occupied by people who partake in varying amounts of both doctrines and beliefs: people who are proudly patriotic about their country *and* believe in the spread of the machine: people who are rigorously orthodox Catholics *and* (following the "Rerum Novarum" encyclical of Pope Leo XIII) believe in curbing the inhumanity of capitalist enterprise and achieving social justice through means that are different only in name from socialism.

131

For the purposes of this discussion, I shall confine myself to the two great collective sources of tradition—religion and nationality. Both of these are embodied in concrete institutions, the Churches and the national community or state; both of them embody and conserve values which men cannot always intellectually define or rationally account for, but values for which men have gladly lived and toiled, for which in the past they have not hesitated to die.

Has tradition still the same hold upon men now as in the past? Plainly not, for that hold has been shaken by many new things. Have the traditionalists made mistakes of commission and omission as serious as those of the pragmatic liberals? Plainly they have. As with the liberals, I purpose to inquire as to what is durable in traditionalism, and what must be discarded, if civilization is to survive.

21. LOVE AMONG THE RUINS

In the Western World the Christian Church has served for more than fifteen hundred years as the chief repository of the values produced by the civilizations that preceded the Church. Much of what has remained of ideal liberalism was transmitted through the Church, at first mechanically, then, thanks to the spirited intercourse that took place with the Arabic culture in the twelfth and thirteenth centuries, through the conscious assimilation of the great scholastic philosophers: above all, John of Salisbury and Thomas Aquinas.

The most valuable bequest from Rome itself derives from Peter's dream and Paul's Roman statesmanship: the belief in universality, as opposed to that tribal exclusiveness which, if it had persisted, would have made Christianity only a sect like the Sadducees, limited to the Jews. Christianity did not speak like the Greeks of Hellenes and Barbarians, or like the Jews of Jew and Gentile: Christianity spoke to all men, in the name of the Son of Man, who was also the Son of God.

From the time of St. Paul, at least, the Church was a missionary organization, composed not of those who only saw the light but of those who sought to spread the light.

133

Mohammedanism, which sprang out of the same Judaeo-Syriac world at a slightly later date, is the only other surviving religion that has a similar zeal and similar drive to keep the faith by widening the circle of the faithful. Buddhism had it at one time, with equal vigor, but has since subsided; while the other missionary cults, like Manicheanism and Mithraism, have long since vanished away. In consequence, the planetary spread of capitalism and Western culture was not due to the pressure of greed alone: for the merchants followed in the wake of the missionaries; and the very first to lead the movement for foreign missions was a saint whose motives not even the most cynical may suspect: St. Francis of Assisi. It was Christianity's claim of universalism that underlay the confident explorations—no less than the rough conquests—of latterday Western imperialism. There was gold to be looted in the new world: but there were also souls to be saved.

Now the Christian Church arose in a period of dwindling vitalities, moral confusion, and economic muddlement. Confronted with a society that was sinking, century by century, into deeper decay, the Christian Church attempted to transcend the dilemmas of this society by showing that the purposes of the pagan world were meaningless, and that all the goods that it purchased so dearly, all the interests that it defended so cumbersomely, were not worth the price. For the Christian it was not Rome, but mortal life itself that was at fault: one must be dead to that life before one could be regenerated. Death itself was not a threat but a promise. So the Church sought to replace men's interests in the here and now and center them on a remote series of ultimate events: the day of judgment: the eternity of punishment or bliss that would be meted out to all men, according to their ability to repent of their earthly sins and find salvation.

Intellectually speaking the theological dogmas of the Christian Church were inacceptable to minds that were well-trained in Greek philosophy. Their appeal lay rather on the emotional level: the various articles of faith might contradict science and common sense, but people believed them triumphantly because they were incredible. Out of the vast rubbish heap of dusty beliefs that constituted the culture of the Roman world, beliefs gathered from every conquered nation, brought back as booty to the imperial capital, the Church created a formal structure of belief. If one took the foundations for granted, the superstructure held together. In this age of agony and disintegration, a belief that held together was more important than a thousand scattered incoherent truths, which no one had the energy to master or the imagination to use in a more creative fashion. Those who had faith could go on. In this fragmentary world heresy—that is another fragment— was a real sin.

Christianity effected certain concrete human results of enormous importance; and some of those results have not

---

lost their meaning even today. This new religion, arising above the shattered Roman world, made it possible for men to confront with stouter hearts the daily miseries, the endless exacerbations, that enveloped them. It could not save this world; that was not its mission; for the energy necessary for worldly salvation, which might have stayed the whole dreadful process in the second century, was no longer in existence by the end of the third century A.D.; the poison of decay had weakened the whole system. Christianity concentrated on that which the Romans refused to face: the inevitability of their disintegration as a society and of their death as individuals. War, slavery, starvation, the spreading ruin of all the old hopes and certainties— that was the medium in which the Christian Church first flourished.

The fact that the Christian Church arose in the classic Time of Troubles has given to Christianity a quality that is rivaled, perhaps, only by Judaism. The latter, too, had two great moments of crystallization, the period of bondage in Egypt, with the flight to Canaan under Moses, and the period of the Babylonian captivity. Israel's tough capacity for survival was due to the fact that in the Babylonian period it invented the synagogue as the communal nexus of Jewish life in both its intellectual and emotional phases; this, and the fact that the most enduring kind of fellowship is that in privation and suffering, have given the Jews their strength.

Christianity was concerned with the agony of Jesus: his death so that all men who partake of his spirit may live again. The myth of Jesus put into more personal, more intimate terms the miracle of the earth's renewal, from season to season and year to year: the death of the vegetation God in winter, with the dying year, and his resurrection in the spring, with the lengthening days. Out of this symbol, now realized in a Person, came Christianity's great capacity for administering to the defeated, the browbeaten, and the hopeless. This faith was at home in the presence of Death: its eyes shone with a starry hope when those of other creeds were dim with tears. "Death is dead, not ye!" Among the barbarian tribes, into the half-deserted cities and the old manor houses where day by day life was becoming coarse and meager, Christianity brought the good word.

As long as the agony of disruption was real, Christianity was the one truly vital force in the Western World. Though it could not halt the process of dissolution, it was the seed from which, after the tenth century, the new life sprouted and pushed through the long-fallow earth once more. In law and custom, the Church carried on the Roman tradition, at a time when every parish had acquired century-old customs that could not be challenged, and retained tribal laws that made no sense in terms of common human purposes. So, by actual inheritance, if not always by intellectual conviction, the Christian religion conserved

137

the essential beliefs of ideal liberalism: the sacredness of truth, justice, freedom. One essential to the moral life had been lacking in that liberal galaxy: love. The stone which the pagan philosophers relegated to an obscure position, was the cornerstone of the new faith: its cornerstone on the earth, and the keystone of its arch in the heavens.

In opposition to the pagan contempt for life, as exhibited in the institution of slavery and the debasing spectacles of the Roman arena, as well as in the ruthless slaying of conquered enemies out of mere lust, the Christian religion proclaimed the sacredness of life. The infinite value of the human personality and the sacredness of human life became an essential element in the structure of Christian faith. Christians might forget that element; they might defile it; but in principle the Church never modified it or abandoned it.

As for the Christian belief in the power of love, it was the very opposite of the barbarian's open love of power. From love spring all the special Christian virtues—mercy, charity, peace—and, above all, the capacity for sacrifice. Nietzsche's contempt for Christianity as the religion of women only mirrored his contempt for women—which was the other side of his almost homosexual adoration of the brutal warrior. Christianity would accept that contempt as a compliment; for even more deeply than Hinduism, which has made the life-giving cow the symbol of the sacred domestic virtues, Christianity has centered on the life-giving, life-continuing, life-sacrificing forces of women. In this sense, every mother is a born Christian: even the father knows that it is only by the capacity to surrender one's own private life for that other life one brings into the world that the race can survive.

There is no creation without this sacrifice. The parent knows it. But so does the poet who turns his back upon an easy job and dedicates himself to lonely days, days of poverty, in order that he may have that abundance of spirit out of which his poems can grow. The false poet slinks into an advertising agency and becomes a cynical breeder of images which deny the very value of life itself. That same potentiality for love, that same capacity for sacrifice, is shown by the miner who risks his life to save his fellows trapped in the mineshaft, by the lineman who risks electrocution to pull a comrade away from a live wire, by the physician who enters the plague-stricken house, by honest, decent men and women everywhere.

Christianity does not depend upon going to Church or observing the Sabbath: both the Sabbath and the Church were made for man, not man for the Sabbath. It is by love and sacrifice that men daily recapture the spirit of Christ.

He who loses his life shall find it. This is the core of Christian faith; but it is far more than that. Only those who act on this principle have a capacity for freedom: for if an individual's life is so dear to him that he will sacrifice anything—betray his friends, renounce the truth, grovel in the dirt—in order to keep his heart pumping and his lungs breathing he is already, for all practical purposes, a slave.

That which in fact distinguishes our Western civilization from the servile, despotic states that so long reigned in other parts of the world is this very realization that life, at its highest and intensest, has nothing to do with the mere maintenance of the physical body. At the moment of saying good-by to that body one may, for the first time, truly live.

Despotism, in other parts of the world, has long battened upon the contemptible weakness of men who do not hold such a faith. Cruelty and brutality are common in the Orient, as necessary supports of despotism, because men have learned to look the other way. I will not say that Christianity has any exclusive claim to this virtue; moral bravery, like moral perception, is not something that one part of the race has patented. But the belief that life must be preserved, not at any cost, but on ideal terms, was a central element in Christ's religion. And the opposite is true: those who seek only their life, shall lose it.

All men die. But only those who know love can endure with unclouded mind, without recrimination and bitterness, the act of sacrifice. It is easy to face giving up life once; one knows the stoicism of the man in the street who says: I'll go when I get my ticket. But he who accepts

Christ's message must give up life daily in order that he may live. Only by an athletic readiness to face absentions, poverties, curtailments of pleasure and power, for the sake of love, can this spirit continue to live.

This is an heroic imposition. The marvel is not that men have often flouted this doctrine even when they solemnly professed it; the marvel is that it has been kept alive by a handful of faithful souls in every generation, even during the periods of unbridled worldliness and corruption within the Christian Church itself.

And the greater marvel is that in periods of crisis, for short spans of time, millions of men and women have been able to live in this spirit. An earthquake, a flood, a war, sometimes rouses this dormant capacity of man to contemn personal annihilation precisely because he wishes life— the life of his children, his neighbors, his fellowmen—to continue endlessly. If this were not so, the human spirit could not have survived the ceaseless corruptions and miscarriages of human purpose. And if our moral flabbiness and self-betrayal have advanced to such a deep stage of decay that it is no longer so, then the human spirit is dead, and what survives it will have only the perverse vitality of a cancer, sure to doom the body that harbors it.

22. REVERSAL OF HUMAN VALUES

As a going institution, Christianity had many sources of political strength and moral power. It had inherited a structure of law and administration; it continued and recast the traditions of architecture, painting, and music that had existed in the classic world. It created an actual physical environment which corresponded to its inner life: the monastery and the cathedral. Between Gregory the Great in the seventh century and Pope John XXII in the fourteenth century, religion had primacy in men's lives: they prayed and fought and planted and built in the conviction that faith moved mountains, not that mountains might obstruct faith.

Such a state of mind is a hard one for modern man to recover; for since the fourteenth century in the Western World a curious upset of values has come about. Without question the majority of modern men accept the notion that economic values are primary ones. They look upon the need for food, clothing, and shelter as a prime mover; and they tend to regard all other institutions merely as transmitters—or transformers—of the original economic energy, at best sublimations and at worst as wasteful diversions.

This belief in our time is a hard one to escape from. Habitually, everyone thinks of our society as being founded on land, resources, power, scientific inventions, industrial and commercial organizations. These things have primacy in our minds; they come first in all our plans and calculations; and if something goes wrong, it is in these departments that people seek the cause.

But that puts the cart before the horse; for the essential fact that sets off human society from those of other creatures, and higher human societies from lower ones, is man's dearly acquired means for communion, for co-operation, for communication. The foundations of society, as such, are law and custom and morals: they are language and literature and the other arts that are needed to convey knowledge and express common feelings: they are all the tried routines and organized usages that promote human co-operation. Some vestige of these capacities may be found in animal groups; but it is only among men that they have been well developed and it is only among civilized men that they have been raised to high degree, and handed on, while the cultures that embodied them rose and fell, for thousands of years.

Our "immaterial" heritage is not without substance: but it needs only a minimum of baggage to go on with its journey. A thousand courtrooms may be destroyed; yet all is saved if only the books of law remain and the traditions are handed on from mouth to mouth; a thousand buildings may be destroyed by fire or incendiary bombs or sheer iconoclasm, but if a few fragments of painting and sculpture remain, and a saving remnant of artists, life will go on again. So with science: so with all the other arts. The material organization and structure remain minimal. That which must be kept alive at all costs is the spirit that creates the laws, the arts, the moral values: this forms as it were the topsoil of civilization; and when it is entirely eroded centuries and even millennia may be needed to recover it.

To say this is to say that religion, ethics, and esthetics are at least as important as science and technology and economic organization: in humility, those who speak for the spirit need say no more. But if any part of our natural or social inheritance is precious, it is that part which man has created and preserved over thousands of years; not that which he seized but yesterday. This is an essential truth in the traditionalist's position; and it is time for it to be re-stated and recognized.

The notion that truth, justice, freedom, and love are foundations of human society, no less than coal and electricity, would not have sounded strange to Socrates or Thomas Aquinas—though their contemporaries were as blind to the meaning of this fact as our own, and the very age that produced Socrates also saw that rabid outbreak of Athenian imperialism against which Euripides nobly protested. If this notion sounds heretical to even the conservative mind today, it is because modern society has re-versed the natural order of thought, which puts our high-est values first, and has thus destroyed the very basis for human dignity and communal integrity.

But let us become aware of the consequences of this per-version. Without respect for truth itself—not for any par-ticular set of truths—the very possibility of human com-munication is vitiated and destroyed. Without freedom there is no possibility of moral choice or voluntary per-sonal loyalty. While without justice, differences of ability, talent, or interest, which are the very basis of the social division of labor, result in the strong taking advantage of the weak, and the unscrupulous preying upon the un-fortunate.

Lacking truth, justice, freedom, a community may have the courage of lions, the infernal resourcefulness of rats, and the perfect social organization of ants; but the mem-bers of it will still not be human. There is nothing in the constitution of the machine to determine what it shall pro-duce, who shall work at it, or how its products should be distributed. The cult of power that the machine has spread through the world has in fact mainly enriched the rich and fortified the powerful.

Those who devoted themselves to inventions thought that a mere abundance of goods would guarantee a better living to everyone. By sheer technical adroitness, they thought that men might avoid the more difficult task of dispensing justice. But just the opposite has happened. Lacking a moral aim, this society cannot even achieve mechanical efficiency. Unused surpluses, idle plants and idle capital, civil war between workers and owners, internecine strife between consumer groups and producing groups—all these things annul the triumphs of invention. And so in the world at large. Without international justice, the conquest of space and time and the worldwide fabric of production have produced only strife, confusion, and vengeful parochialism.

Material organization, then, is no substitute for moral order. The final test of an economic system is not the tons of iron, the tanks of oil, or the miles of textiles it produces: the final test lies in its ultimate products—the sort of men and women it nurtures, and the order and beauty and sanity of their communities. Divorced from a system of moral and esthetic values, the most powerful industrial organization or political state completely lacks human validity.

23. THE DE-MORALIZATION OF ECONOMICS

Let me give a single illustration of our present social plight—the divorce between economics and ethics. This finally led to that reversal of values which puts economics first and makes ethics take second place, as an outsider, or refuses to give it houseroom at all.

Up to the thirteenth century, thanks to the Church, economic life existed under the same dispensation as every other part of existence. Honest labor occupied a high place in the Christian ethic, and the Fathers of the Church did not believe that saintliness was, without a special vocation, an excuse for not earning one's daily bread. To labor was to pray.

But those who were occupied with earning a living, and in particular those who bought and sold, were subject to special temptations: the sins of usury, avarice, and greed. While people who occupied positions of social responsibility and economic authority were open, in a special degree, to the further sins of luxury and pride. This is not to say that these sins did not exist in the Middle Ages, along with all the usual run of faults and crimes and perversities: quite the contrary. One has only to accompany Dante through his Inferno to discover this.

147

But the very recognition of sin as sin means that no one mistakes it for a value or a virtue. It means that those who accept the standard have the obligation to resist sin in themselves and to fight against it in others.

First in fact, then in theory, this moral code was overthrown by the rise of capitalism. As early as the fourteenth century Pope John XXII denounced as heretics those followers of St. Francis who professed that the early Christians had renounced private property and held everything in common. The Church persecuted the heretical Waldensians for this reason, as well as for more purely theological diversions from orthodoxy; and again, what gave impetus to the Lollards in England and the Hussites in Bohemia was their insistence that greed of gain—Lady Meed, as the author of "Piers Plowman" called it—was a denial of Christian principle.

Why did the Catholic Church give ground to the new capitalistic doctrines? Plainly its own needs as a powerful organization, commanding vast wealth, poisoned the will to resist. Calvin, two centuries later, only carried out into clear-cut doctrine the Catholic Church's earlier counsels of expediency. For the new capitalist, the deadly sins, as catalogued by the Christian Church, had become the cardinal virtues. Avarice was thrift, which led to the accumulation of capital. Usury was the reward not only for risk but for deferred enjoyment: the parallel in life to the deferred enjoyment of earthly pleasures which was to be consummated in Heaven. Luxury was no less a virtue in the new scheme: it became the very motive power for production.

But the supreme virtue, in this transvaluation of Christian values, was pride. Though the Church, in its real wisdom, regarded pride as the worst of sins, it now became the very pillar of the economic and political order. It was pride in wealth that made the great wholesale guilds draw away from the petty handicraft guilds. It was pride that stirred the conquistadors and freebooters of the sixteenth century or the imperialists of the nineteenth; it was pride in class that grew with the means of exploitation, and pride in birth that made the European think that his very white complexion was in some sense an absolute value, giving him the privilege of looking down on the colored races. (They have had their revenge: it is now a point of pride with the leisure classes to have a skin the year round as dark, at least, as a Polynesian!)

National pride entered likewise: a new form of collective egoism. In time this national pride was sufficient, in Germany and England, to challenge the power of Rome, and to transfer the seat of ecclesiastical authority from the Tiber to the countries it had once spiritually governed. Such national pride magnifies the individual ego a thousand diameters: it encourages people to do collective homage to the inflated image of self without being convicted of madness and imbecility.

Finally, pride in man's power over nature grew. That

pride sufficed to wipe out primitive peoples, to wreck and devitalize regional landscapes; in the end it conjured up vast elemental forces derived from his knowledge of physics and chemistry—forces which man has still not the moral capacity to use without inflicting damage upon himself.

The fantastic pride of modern man in his own instruments and his own spoliations has kept him from seeing the real nature of his triumphs. Half of the goods he claimed as his own invention he had filched, almost unconsciously, from the more primitive peoples he exploited. How was Western man enabled to multiply so rapidly during the nineteenth century? In large part because of his taking over from the Amerinds of the New World their great horticultural discoveries, potatoes and maize and beans: four-sevenths of the world's food production today. And from whom did he acquire one of his most precious arts, the art of using rubber: responsible for a thousand indispensable products, from rubber tires to contraceptives? That art came from the primitive tribes in the Brazilian jungle; the people who had invented the rubber ball, the rubber syringe, and the rubber raincoat. In short, modern technology itself is the result, not of this nation's art or that continent's wealth, but of the collaboration of mankind.

But pride comes before a fall: that lesson is one on which the wisdom of the Jews, the Greeks, and the Christians agree. Out of the European's reckless delight in conquering nature and subduing the less savage peoples of the earth, he created the massive injustices of imperialism; he produced resentment in the conquered and callousness in those who ruled; so that the mondial co-operations that were becoming effective toward the end of the nineteenth century were already spoiled, as Herbert Spencer astutely saw, by the rise of a Servile State. Thanks to the older traditions of freedom, that state was challenged and in part curbed in England, France, and the United States; but the evil precedent remained at work.

Presently, fascism took form, and the tide which was ebbing away in other countries came back with redoubled destructive force. Now it carried with it the notion, not of making Western man governor of the more primitive peoples, but of creating a conquering people, self-chosen to rule, who with a monopoly of the means of violence would in good time govern the earth. There was no longer any question of trade, even the one-sided trade of imperialism: the master nation, according to Hitler and his followers, will live in style off the tribute and slave labor of the inferior peoples it has conquered.

Here is the ultimate form of pride: the complete parasitism of the powerful. Who will deny that it has its equivalent in so-called democratic countries among the possessors of wealth, in particular among the second and third generations that have inherited riches without having either

151

the will or the skill to accept active social responsibility.

In other words, the development of economic enterprise, in a world without religious or ethical values, must lead eventually to a destructive or parasitic economy, either one bent on increasing the riches of the powerful, by any means available, from working pauper children fourteen hours a day as was once done in England to exterminating rivals by bribing officers of the law and hiring gunmen; or else one bent on achieving safety and effortless indulgence, by making use of the law to secure monopoly in one of its many forms. The final result, one may remark, is usually as uneconomic as it is unethical; for the very nature of trade, if it is to be founded on a permanent basis, is a give-and-take between equals, in which each party gains, but neither has a formal advantage over the other.

This de-moralization of economics had still another outcome. It wiped out the claim of religion to govern either economic or political life. And what is left for religion after that claim is liquidated? Little more than a brief code for mating, a ceremonial for marriage, chicken broth and visitation for the ill, and a few seemly words and gestures at the burial service. The one-sided development of the industrial world turned religion into an effeminate triviality. The time and effort of modern men, for the last two centuries, have been largely spent on matters outside the pale of religious doctrine: affairs that were at best indifferent to religion and at worst openly hostile. Religion, in other words, became very much like kingship as described by Mark Twain: it made a great noise and show, but it was simply not connected with the works. Religion was something to think about all day and never do; and after a while, a great part of the population refused even the hypocrisy of thinking about it.

Instead of morals curbing and directing the great engines of power we have created, power has demoralized life. The ultimate product of that de-moralization is fascism: for fascism does, with all the conviction it can muster, what the rest of the world has always done somewhat ineffectively, because of a divided mind. For a few centuries mankind was freed from the worst effects of Machiavellianism by the fact that the Church, even when it, too, was seizing power, had created a ceremonial of hypocrisy: velvet gloves on the iron hand. Now the gloves are gone. No holds are barred. Under those rules there is every chance that the worst side will win.

24. CAPITALISM CONNIVES AT SUICIDE

Since there is no connection in the modern mind between economic purposes and ethical norms, capitalism has exposed the final weakness of those who possess neither human values nor ethical purposes: it cannot defend *itself*. That is one of the paradoxes of the present situation.

This paradox has been hidden, perhaps, because the communists have invented a fable about the nature of fascism to make it accord with their one-sided version of economic determinism. With them, it is fashionable to picture fascism as the last desperate phase of monopoly capitalism, as an attempt on the part of capitalists to use violence to stay in power. There is no doubt about the violence; but that capitalists stay in power is questionable. Except for a few pet capitalists, personal friends and close accomplices of the gang at the top, power is transferred under fascism from the financial centers to the party bureaucracy. That is what happens from within.

But in the democracies something far worse, something far more grotesque, happens. Because profit is the be-all and end-all of production under capitalism, the capitalists in democratic countries have not been willing to pay the taxes for munitions and armament that would ensure their protection against foreign assault. They sought to arm at bargain counter rates against a foe that strained every fibre day and night to equip himself: a foe that sacrificed far more than butter to get his tanks and planes. More than this: politicians and business men have shown an uncanny willingness to do business with the very foreign powers that were out to destroy their country. I do not refer merely to England and France: our record in the United States is quite as bad. Instead of cutting off the supply of machine tools and scrapiron and oil to the totalitarian powers, our rulers have armed our enemies. In the smaller countries like Holland and Belgium the utter incapacity of the privileged groups to accept the need for sacrifice— which was both a moral imperative and the bare demand for self-preservation—made capitalists the silent partners of the Nazis.

At the same time this policy increased the resentment and the distrust of the industrial workers, who saw no reason to forego their modest privileges if the capitalist classes were unwilling to curb their enormous ones. Unready to risk either their lives or their properties, these financiers, industrialists, and landlords will presently lose both; for their property will be valueless in a disorganized world, even if their fascist masters let them retain it, while their lives, even from their own philistine standpoint, will be worth less.

This incapacity upon the part of the men of business

and industry to face the realities of the fascist world puts them in the same group as the political and intellectual liberals—wishful thinkers all, pursuing obstinately a policy of wishful waiting, believing on each occasion that they make another appeasement or another surrender that this time it will be "different." Like the proverbial dog, they return patiently to their vomit. Or rather, they are like the drowning man in Ruskin's mordant illustration who is actually brought nearer to death by the heavy money-belt around his waist.

This ultimate de-moralization of our economic society would not have surprised a Kropotkin, a Thoreau, a Tolstoy, or a Morris, different though their several philosophies of life were. Lacking moral values, capitalism lacks the power to survive. In national affairs the business men of the democratic countries have so far showed themselves to be poltroons: they are the counterparts of those chicken hearted American business men who do not dare to risk damage to their property or loss of their lives when threatened with the extortions of gangsters. Such people lack even a sense of honor as business men. People who are so demoralized could not even be counted upon as reliable confederates in a gang of thieves; at least there is honor among thieves. Or perhaps one should say, there used to be.

Once ethics are pushed aside, the foundations of human society begin to slip and slide: this is what it comes to.

156

At that point, the choice between cannibalism and vegetarianism becomes only a matter of taste, as the Russian premier said of the difference between communism and fascism. Those very words of course betray the user of them. For in a society where values are still alive, taste itself involves more than the tongue and the palate of a single individual: it involves standards that have existed before him, that will be modified by him, and that will be subject to future modification precisely because the social background itself remains in existence.

25. TEMPTATIONS OF THE CHURCHES

In view of what has happened these last centuries, it would seem that a powerful case could be made out for religion, as a necessary binding force in society; and for Christianity in particular, because it has often been able to summon up the spirit of sacrifice. But the case is not so simple as that: for the Churches have, by and large, been no less disloyal to their ideal traditions than have the pragmatic liberals. And as with every other institution in the modern world, a process of sub-surface erosion has been going on in the domain of religion whose evil results are now, almost for the first time, fully visible.

The critical weakness of the Christian Church is that it has lost universality. This has happened in two ways: the original schism between the Western and the Eastern Churches has been multiplied by fissures and cleavages between the various Protestant sects; and these sects, as in a mica-rock, have split off into even smaller fragments. In addition to that, the very age of exploration, which sent the Church out on far-flung missionary enterprises, has only proved how far Christianity is from being a universal religion: the Hindu and the Mohammedan religions are also in existence. A true Catholicism must be

158

as broad as the mind of an Emerson; it must embrace the
experience and culture of the East no less than the West;
indeed, as he suggested, it must contain the skepticisms as
well as the beliefs of humanity. The myth of Christ is a
great myth; but so is the myth of Brahma. The ethic of
Jesus is a supreme ethic; but in the same category is the
ethic of the Bhagavad-Gita.

Partly through historical and partly through geopolitical
causes, the Christian Church has become sectarian, parochial; and though it has much to give the other religions
of the earth, the notion that the form it has so far assumed
is a final one would mean either that the Church was dead,
or that Heaven had come upon earth.

But the Church has become parochial in an even narrower sense: it has attached itself to the national state
and has become the official cult of its ruling class. At first
this was true only of the Church of England and the Lu-
theran Church; both cases involved a degradation in spiritual authority, and a transferal of allegiance to an earthly
king, who distributed benefices and expected payment in
kind. But by now it is equally true of the Church that
claims direct succession through Saint Peter to Jesus
Christ. The largest single body of practicing Christians,
those in the Roman faith, are subject to the political exigen-
cies of a single country. The Pope of Rome is now always
an Italian; the cardinals, the ruling council of the Church,
are preponderantly Italian; and in order to preserve this

narrow national bias, the upper members of the hierarchy must get their higher training in Rome: no one who seeks to advance beyond a monsignor can avoid that training.

Under these conditions, the Church's pretense to universality is pathetic. It rises above narrow national obsessions only as an imperial power does, by attempting to subject other nations to the same influences as its own nationals. And as the moral authority of the Church has decreased, now that it neither commands free loyalty nor exercises effective power through excommunication, its dependence upon the support of the state has become more abject. In its desire for power, the Catholic Church plays with the powerful; and in its disregard for human brotherhood it sanctifies the idols of the tribe: as it happens today, Mussolini's tribe, Hitler's tribe.

Political interpreters have set various dates for the beginning of the fascist uprising against civilization; but most of them go back no farther than 1931. This is a curious blindness: the betrayal of the Christian world, very plainly, took place in 1928, in the Concordat that was made between Mussolini and the Pope. That made political Catholicism the partner of fascism; and as events turned out in Spain, no silent partner. It was this that opened the way for the sinister issues that followed; for the turning over of Germany to the Brown Shirts was accomplished, after the deposition of Bruening, by another Catholic, Von Papen, on the assumption that the Church and the fascists would make common cause against communism—against communism in theory, but against the Weimar Republic and *against world democracy* in fact.

Undoubtedly the Church has paid for acting as an accomplice here: one by one Hitler has stripped it of its powers in Germany, and he has smashed out of existence the very memory of some of the most devout communities in Poland. But what matters it to the politicians of the Italian Church if it lose Northern Europe, always somewhat doubtfully within the grasp of Rome, and gain the whole world? If the outposts of Franco's Spain can be successfully extended to Latin America, as he purposes, and if Mussolini grabs at least a lapdog's share of Africa, fascist Catholicism will then be in a position to put the screws on North America, too. Patriotic American Catholics may well deny that they have any such aim, or that the Church has; but blatherskites like Father Coughlin have, in their overweening self-confidence, already let the cat out of the bag. If the democratic forces in America threaten to curb the political powers of the so-called "Christian Front," that is, Catholic fascism, this seditious priest has threatened to do what the fascist Spaniards did: call in foreign aid.

It should be plain, I trust, that I am not assailing the religious and ethical doctrines of Christianity: they are part of mankind's treasure, and even those outside the Church are deeply in debt for their existence. What I am talking about is the politics of a church dominated by an Italian hierarchy, and pursuing, with its fine Italian hand, a scheme of conquest which will give the major political power, if successful, to those authoritarian forms of government which best comport with its own plans and purposes. Unfortunately the aims of fascism are most deeply in conflict with those of a free republic like that of the United States. In this effort, the Catholic Church has been plainly no conservator of tradition: it has been an ally—and a potent ally—of the forces of destruction.

When one turns to Protestantism, the case is little better, though the weakness and corruption have been of a different kind. With the Protestant Church the evil has derived, not so much from political ambition, as from a failure to accept political responsibility. Historically, the Protestant Church grew up at a moment when the breach between politics, economics, and morals had fully opened. The emphasis upon purely personal salvation left the individual free in the world of business to behave with harsh rationalism, untempered by any of the gentler virtues. Protestantism has served the middle classes, who wished to keep themselves to themselves; and no one would deny that the heart of the Catholic priesthood has often been much closer to the needs of the humbler workers.

The social irresponsibility of Protestantism comes out precisely in those features of doctrine which stress its purity. The Wesleyan concern for grace and its holy desire to awaken emotional fervor were, for example, a little too innocent: or rather, they ignored too easily the ugly environment, the sordid aims, the relentless illiberality, that were typical of the period of evangelical revivalism. Emotion was precisely what was lacking in the environment of Coketown: all manner of art or polite living had been gutted out of the new industrial towns. The Wesleyans turned on this pious emotion as a bartender might pour out gin—and for the same reason: it was the quickest way of getting out of Manchester.

This applies likewise to the pacifism that the Protestant Churches have preached, ever more volubly since the first World War. Such pacifism is politically too unambitious: the Jesus who taught peace also carried a whip to drive the money changers out of the temple. Pacifism, as we have seen in discussing the pragmatic liberals, may be an excuse for moral inertia. The social irresponsibility of the Christian Churches cannot be overcome by lip-service. Mere verbal devotion to the higher ends of life, at Sunday services or midweek prayer meetings—with picnics or strawberry festivals at odd times—brings with it little of the stern discipline needed to face the present world. Orthodox Protestantism, before the middle of the nineteenth century, was built of tougher materials; and I do not hesitate to say that it produced better men and women. There was a terrible elevation in Jonathan Edwards: there is a complacent pedestrianism in most Protestant preachers

163

today. With honorable exceptions aside, they are as a class the last group to which anyone would go for rigorous spiritual counsel, man to man. In the pulpit they conceal their weakness because they are actors, and have learned their lines.

Perhaps the final comment on Protestantism as a spiritual force today must be attached to the teaching of one of the most unctuous of evangelical preachers, the founder of a worldwide movement that claims millions of adherents. This gentleman has carried Protestant anarchism to its logical conclusion: the hope of using a dictator like Hitler in order to place the world under "God control." Such a creed begins by elevating the individual and ends by sanctioning a despot who deliberately defiles the temple of the human personality. One hardly knows which is more contemptible: the betrayal of democracy or the sleek debauchery of Christianity that makes it possible.

In one final weakness within the Church both Catholic and Protestant share: their inability to recognize as religious those contemporary manifestations of religion that take other than the old familiar forms. If you ask a churchman to name the great religious painters of modern times, he will probably answer, if he is a cultivated person, that there have been no great religious painters; or he will mention some nonentity who has painted aureate oleaginous pieties that need a wash of vinegar before one looks at them. But there have been two outstanding religious

164

painters within the last sixty years: van Gogh and Rouault. Van Gogh, as both a man and an artist, had qualities that bind him to the great saints of the past; but it is not through the Churches that one will discover this fact.

The same holds true in literature. There have been great artists, like Balzac and Dostoyevsky, who remained within the circle of Christian orthodoxy; there have been others, like the author of "Les Fleurs du Mal," who returned to it: these men were steeped in the religious tradition. But this is not the same thing as saying that the Church itself has recognized the spiritual value of the works produced by these men: that the Orthodox Russian priest turned to "The Idiot" or "The Possessed" to have a deeper insight into the moral dilemmas and psychological whirlpools of the time, or that the Catholic Church has utilized Balzac's vast panorama of human life, centered around the pride and avarice and greed of bourgeois France, as the modern equivalent—which it is—for the simple morality plays that used to be enacted on the porch of the Church.

This irresponsiveness to the creative thought of the world for the last three hundred years has not merely drained the Church of many live minds, but has compelled the living to seek for spiritual nutriment outside the Church. The diet has been abundant; there has been no real falling off in spiritual vitality if one appraises the effort as a whole. But it has been a sort of buffet supper for the soul: in which people sometimes get too many helpings of what is not good for them, and are passed over, by accident, when something particularly fine is going the rounds.

There is need for discrimination and order: such discrimination and order as an organized institution can build up by continued service. By refusing to recognize thought or imagination this side of the seventeenth century as tradition, the Church, again, has betrayed tradition. Our religion should be a repository for the best that has been thought, felt, imagined, divined, in each age: but it is rather like a bank that will accept no more deposits because it does not know a safe business in which it may invest its capital. Such an institution must presently go bankrupt; one cannot effectively keep the possessions that one has unless one has the courage to put them in circulation and devote them to fresh enterprises and adventures.

This is not to say that a religion should compromise its ideal values: just the contrary. The chief mission of organized religion is to keep alive, through all the tribulations and frustrations of actual living, those ideal points of reference without which human life becomes savage, degraded, and brutish. Herman Melville put this problem very keenly in a chapter in "Pierre," in which his mystical philosopher, Plinlimmon, discusses the difference between Greenwich time and local time, between an otherworldly ethics and the practical standards of a going community.

166

In order to keep time properly with the aid of chronometers and watches, it is necessary to have a fixed observatory, which serves as an absolute point of reference. Local time is, by agreement, relative to Greenwich time. There is nothing more meaningless to a person off the meridian of Greenwich than to give him the time in Greenwich terms without telling his longitude and his distance in minutes and hours from Greenwich. To hold that Greenwich time is enough by itself as a guide is the mistake of the abstract idealist. But local time, which has no other point of reference than its own watches—and lacks any observatories capable of astronomical reckoning— has no way of determining how well the watches run, whether they are gaining or losing.

The problem for social man is to keep his reckonings in accord with Greenwich time. This does not demand that each man should live at Greenwich himself and become an Astronomer Royal. But it means that relative measurements must not themselves be treated as absolutes.

In departing from the absolutes of religion, modern man made precisely this last error. Instead of looking for better astronomical observations, for some more inclusive system than Christianity itself, he discarded the very habit of looking at the heavens; he assumed that as long as he could manufacture watches and provide everyone with them, he might forget those more ultimate calculations. He took for granted that religion had nothing to teach him; that its eternal search for perfection was meaningless; that its concern for the permanent, the durable, the traditional—in an historic sense, the absolute—values of life was unworthy of a race that had timed the speed of light, and was marching steadily to new mechanical triumphs: air-conditioned houses and bomb-proof shelters.

One grants that the ancient wisdom of religion is quantitatively minute; scarcely more bulky than the few grains of radium preserved in the cancer hospital. But though man knows very little about either himself or his estate the universal distinction that all religions have made between good and evil, between truth and error, between long-time tendencies and wayward impulses, is part of the little that man actually knows. One may be able to chart the course of an electric charge, split an atom, imitate a thunderbolt, or send six hundred messages simultaneously through the same cable; but unless one knows in addition that good and evil are constant realities in human life, all one's other intellectual acquisitions are worthless. The consciousness of this truth turns the trifler into a responsible personality. Without it, the cancer of evil may work its way uncontrolled through human society, until corruption and death are everywhere.

If we dispense with ideal standards, in short, all our clocks go wrong; indeed the faster the works turn, the greater the error; just as the greater the vitality of the cancer cells the more swiftly the disease eats into the system. The divorce of the practical and relative world of daily living from the astronomical sense of the high religions is surely one of the ultimate causes of the breakdown that has been going on so fast in our own generation. And it is absurd to suppose that one-sided economic prescriptions can overcome this defect; such prescriptions are themselves only symptoms of the disease itself, rather than ways of treating the disease. They are no less remote and fussily futile than those old-fashioned clerical declarations that solemnly announced the time at Greenwich without indicating the local longitude or even knowing what day of the week it was.

One might sum up this observation by saying that our practical institutions will not really be practical unless our ideal institutions are really ideal. There must always be a tension between the two. And if nothing would be more fatal to our daily living than to assume for a moment that eternal values can actually displace relative ones, nothing could be more fatal to our ideals than to make them up-to-date, and make them conform to local customs, local prejudices. Life is significant because it has the capacity for striving toward the ideal: but ideals are vital and valuable precisely because they can never finally be achieved. "For it is provided in the essence of things," as Walt Whitman said, "that from any fruition of success, no matter what, shall come forth something to make a greater struggle necessary."

169

26. COUNSEL IN A TIME OF TROUBLES

So much for the weaknesses of one of the main pillars of the human tradition, our historic religions. Yet if the inner dry rot of Christianity has not gone too far, this faith carries over from its past the very spirit that is necessary to confront a Time of Troubles like the present one.

The qualities that distinguish historic Christianity are those that the modern world has been losing: qualities to which the fascist parties purpose openly to give the final *coup de grâce*. First, Christianity opposes to the parochial and the tribal the sense of a universal mission and a universal brotherhood between all men of good will. To all such it promises that measure of concord which is the fruit of love. This has no guarantee of permanence in political life, any more than in marriage; but it may be perpetually recovered and reinstated.

Again, Christianity accords to all men that equality as whole personalities for which the present political name is democracy. It presumes a community of equals aiming at the best life possible, a community in which minor differences of wealth, vitality, energy, racial inheritance, cultural tradition, other accidental characters, will make no difference in the political and moral status of the person.

It was, indeed, the failure to make good this assumption in the realm of politics that bogged the Christian Church down, first as an ally of a brutal feudalism, then as a defender of reactionary privileges and vested interests in capitalism, and now—at least in the "Catholic" Church of Italy—as an ally of a deliberately sacrilegious and man-exterminating fascism.

Finally, most significant of all, Christianity embraces the facts of birth, love, sacrifice, death, as the constant groundwork of human experience. All these experiences, instead of remaining as isolated events in nature, become for those who understand the Christian vision the very substance and structure of personal and social life. Birth, in this view, is not just the physical departure from the mother's womb: it embraces the other crises of life: the constant re-births of purpose and vision that are necessary if the soul is not to be paralyzed by calcareous deposits of habit.

Birth is the capacity to depart from the old and to confront the new: to leave father and mother and dear ones and push forth on an untrodden trail: to overcome the inertia of the well-tried career and answer the call of the moment, whatever it be. Life is thus, for those who are not content with their more limited and transient selves, a series of re-births: the birth of self-consciousness at adolescence, the birth of selfless devotion in the experience of falling in love; the birth of responsible effort without

171

reward in the development of the maturer self that arises with parenthood and the hard duties of middle life.

Such a re-birth goes on perpetually within a happy marriage; and it is one of the reasons, in every true mating, for desiring a life-span together, so that each crisis of life may provide for love a new birthday. A great musician came to his wife on her deathbed; and one who saw them reported: "There was a look in his eye as if for the first time he was beholding the girl he loved." That was the consummation of a marriage that had lasted almost half a century. Man truly lives by scrapping and rebuilding his dead selves—which is to say, by being born again. This holds as much for communities as for personalities.

So with the other Christian qualities. Love is not the narrow possessiveness that is the first mark of sexual attraction. It awakens perhaps with the original sense of intimacy and devotion to kin within the family group, or in the attraction of mate for mate. But instead of stopping short with erotic fulfillment and returning upon itself, it spreads over into every other field of life, breaking down walls and fences, giving to comradeship and to friendship pledges no less real than those which the married exchange.

Death, finally, in this religious view is not just a peremptory choking off of life. Life spreads benign wings over every act of voluntary sacrifice, from going without food in order that the hungry may be fed to resigning a cherished private ambition in order to serve one's country. All such prunings away of stem and leaf only ensure a fuller efflorescence of life itself. Death, in all the purposive forms of renunciation and sacrifice, translates into socially significant terms the elemental fact of biological death: a making way for life. In its exuberance, unchecked life would gorge itself with its own vitality: the herring, if all their spawn remained alive, would presently fill up the sea; or the flies, if unchecked by death, would form a devastating film of insects over the land.

All that the Christian religion has brought with it, out of a past far remoter than Christianity itself, adds to the depth of its perceptions on the ultimate issues of death and birth. Its strength lies in the fact that it says yes to death as well as to life; and if it brings death into life it also rallies the forces of life and gives them the power, by the very act of anticipation, to surmount death.

Today, a Time of Troubles has again overtaken mankind: a time of individual disintegration and collective disaster. Death—or the imminent possibility of death—or that dreadful exhaustion which is but a suspended death—is the specter that stalks across the blasted fields and gun-rimmed cities of Europe and lurks in the heart of every man and woman on the planet.

At this moment words that have long been empty of meaning come back to life. And a Church that taught one part of mankind to walk upright and unafraid through one

Dark Age may yet summon up the power that will enable us to avert another Dark Age, or to face it, if it begin to descend upon us, with unyielding courage.

But to perform that mission the spirit of sacrifice, and the act of re-birth, must manifest themselves in the Church —above all, in the Church. If it hungers for temporal power it will abet the dark maniacs who now seek to govern the world. And if it seeks peace alone, peace without justice, peace without humanity, it will be fascism's blind accomplice in a crime committed against both the human and the divine.

27. THE NATIONAL BEING

Western civilization knows only one religion that compares in scope and vitality with the main body of the traditional religions. This is the religion of nationalism. Even more than the Church, nationalism has given to the inhabitants of every country and region a common body of faith: belief in a common past, hope for a common future. Very few people have been persecuted for their belief in Christianity during the past century; the cause of nationalism has produced a legion of martyrs and saints: men who have lived selflessly for their nation and have died, like Padraic Pearse and his comrades in the first Irish Revolution, in order that his nation might live.

Nationalism is often treated as a political phenomenon of the same order as socialism. But the fact is that its roots are much deeper; and the sources that feed it are those remote and subtle elements in the soul that bring together in a curious kinship those who laugh at the same kind of joke or pronounce with the same inflection and modulation the words of their language. Nationalism may be defined as the bond of common purpose that unites those who have the same language, the same background of nature, the same rituals of life: one or all of these is necessary, but the patch of earth is all but indispensable, and a common speech—a dialect rather than a language—is part of it. Clusters of emotion form about such ways and objects.

Now the individuality of groups of men is as genuine a fact as personality itself. Of old the inhabitants of Boeotia were slow and the Athenians quick; the Italians were subtle and polished and the Germans uncouth; the French volatile and the English steady. As with all living personalities, groups too change their characters: the bloodthirsty Norsemen who spread terror throughout Europe in the ninth century are today the peaceful Scandinavians who dismantle their armies and offer Peace Prizes. But the sense of group identity, preserved and fortified through historic memories, is the very essence of nationalism. This was true before nationalism had taken on a political rôle; it will remain true, though the apparatus of democratic political life be shattered. He who uproots nationality kills personality.

The nation has had two opposing forces to contend with during the past century. One was the development of those rationalizing habits of mind and those impersonal mechanical organizations which ruthlessly pushed the personal life to one side. In that attack, the nation suffered no less than the individual; but by the very rigors of repression, the nation developed the capacity to resist and to hit back; so that the very century which saw the spread of all the unifying mechanisms, railroads, cables, radios, also saw the unprecedented re-birth of national languages and national literatures. Folk legends, once forgotten, came to light again. Folk costumes were revived; folk dances recovered. A sense of national self-respect led to creative efforts in all the arts. Standish O'Grady in Ireland restored the heroes of the Red Branch and Deirdre of the Sorrows: Emerson, with eyes turned to the future, hailed The American Scholar: Herzl renewed the ancient dreams of Zion.

The rationalist, utilitarian minds of the past generation treated these national revivals as largely reactionary phenomena. If they had any political significance, according to such a view, it was merely as a disguise to the naked search for power in the new states that sought to be unified and politically strong. But reaction itself is a question-begging word, like revolution: the question is always what one is reacting from, or what one is throwing off. Nationalism was a reassertion of group personality, in the face of organized impersonality. In this sense, it was not an alternative to rationalist cosmopolitanism; it was rather a corrective. Both forces were necessary, a universalizing process, and a localizing, regionalizing, nationalizing process. The machine spread modern culture; nationalism assimilated and absorbed modern culture, taking what it could use, modifying it, mixing it with the old, acclimating it to the local scene.

The other inimical element lay within nationalism itself.

177

This was the tendency to identify the national and the local with the interests of the state. In the case of England that state contained nations as conscious of their identity as the Scotch, the Irish, and the Welsh; in the case of a country like America, it led to an attempt to identify as American a particular set of political institutions, which spread over a continent of great diversity. Love of country, love of one's folk, are both very deep elements in the human psyche; but they were thinned out in order to provide motive-power for political and economic combinations that occupied the rulers of the modern state. Local industries might be sacrificed in order to increase the profits of distant shareholders, seeking a national market.

One further result followed. By treating national boundaries as military walls, each national government came to assert an attitude of jealous belligerency against other national governments. The wall itself engendered a non-co-operative spirit in those behind the wall. If political nationals had much in common, they had it mainly in opposition to other sovereign nationalities. So national self-respect was turned into belligerent self-assertion. And so the innocent emotions and feelings which bind men to their village, with its familiar landmarks and familiar faces, were canalized into fuel tanks of emotional suspicion and hatred directed against other nations.

In this new mythology, the nation became god; and the state assumed the position claimed by the Church, as God's representative on earth. But the god was a tribal god, a jealous god: a god who grew strong on the strife that existed between nations. This paranoiac nationalism, with its absurd claims to uniqueness and greatness of its own chosen people, with its intense fear and hatred of all rival nationalities, was but the pathological overstimulation of feelings and perceptions that were, in origin, entirely sound. Such paranoia prepared for war and throve on the very idea of war. By the same token, it denied value to all the unifying instruments and institutions that promised to make men at home wherever they walked or traveled on earth.

National paranoia reaches its final state of disintegration in fascism. As hatred mounts and power grows, the ruling nation, no longer confined to its native soil, no longer content with self-cultivation, seeks to blot out every other nation. At that moment of frenzied self-worship, no sacrifice is too great for the leader to demand of his followers, no humiliation is too base for them to inflict on their victims.

Now the truth is that the nations of the world are no more self-sufficient, no more independent, no more isolated, than the individual personality. They are the focus of energies and ideas that lie far outside their national boundaries both in space and in time. By imagining themselves self-sufficient, by clinging to a myth of isolation, they actually encompass their own doom.

For the principle of nationality can live only in a world where every political unit has a local center, an intimate focus, in the human region, and an outer boundary that is as wide as the world itself. Isolation is suicide. Too late the nations of Europe have found that out; they are now overrun by an aggressive mechanism that by its very nature attacks their personal existence as nations. Given as much as a decade of Nazi rule, the old nations of Europe will be so completely broken up by mass migrations and mass interchanges, that the very possibility of sustained identity will be wiped out.

Political nationalism has thus destroyed the very sources of cultural nationalism. In its arrogance and its pride, in its contempt for other nationalities, in its exorbitant egoisms, it has blindly contrived the ruin of all that men traditionally hold dear: their homes, the sweet sound of a neighbor's greeting, the green earth over which their feet have made a path, or the church steps their ancestors rounded down before they themselves were born. The isolated nations have been traitors to themselves when they deserted each other: when the American Republic deserted the Spanish Republic, when the British and French deserted the Czechs, and the Poles attacked them: when the Dutch refused to co-operate with the British, when the Norwegians and the Swedes and Danes refused to band together in union. All these desertions and treasons were forms of self-desertion and self-betrayal. Unified, surrendering their petty egos and their private sovereignties, the democratic states could have created a powerful engine of justice which would have removed forever the blot of war. Isolated, surrendering one by one, nationalism has given a free hand to the anti-nations. Thus nationalism accomplished the ultimate negation of the national personality: collective suicide.

This is the end of nationalism as a religion. But it is not the end of the national being, not even in Europe: decades of oppression will be needed to wipe out the last trace of these national personalities, since they die like a great tree, from the crown down, and even when the trunk is blasted and barkless, from the base new shoots may arise, capable of overcoming the plague that has killed the main stem. But the isolated nation is a figment of pride: a base delusion. Men are brothers. In the end even fascism will discover that brothers cannot be separated. No nation can long conserve its own traditions unless it has equal respect for all other nations, and will regard every act of violence against them as a personal offense.

28. THE CHALLENGE
OF NON-EUCLIDEAN POLITICS

During the last century, certain mathematicians proved that a whole system of geometry could be constructed on the axiom that parallel lines *do* meet. The set of axioms that were once thought self-evident could be rejected: a new system could be based on just the opposite set of rules.

The fascists have brought about a similar change in politics. They carried to the logical limit the new cult of power. In the face of all human experience, they assumed that politics and industry could be completely divorced from morals. Not merely do the fascist dictators deny the ethical postulates of society; they have created a system with a reverse set of values. In this system fraud is better than truth and can no longer be distinguished from it; violence is better than persuasion, ignorance is better than knowledge provided it augments power, and hate is better than love.

Their system is consistent and self-enclosed. And because, once one grasps the premises, the new order is entirely coherent, it has enabled the fascists in every political situation during the last decade to act with unqualified success. They do exactly what they say they are going to do. And their opponents make the deadly mistake of not believing that the fascists mean what they say, because they do not realize that the fascists have discarded the very axioms upon which all decent human societies, no matter how faulty, have been based.

Thus when Hitler has talked peace with his victims and denounced war-mongers, he has meant war, and those he has called war-mongers were those who proposed to resist him. When he has talked about improving the conditions of the workers, he has meant their enslavement. When he has talked about liberation he has meant conquest, and when he has used the term "protection" he has meant destruction. So, again, when Hitler pledged himself to respect neutrality and agree to non-aggression pacts his pledge was the preliminary to exactly the opposite move. Once one has this key, one can translate any fascist declaration on sight.

This non-Euclidean politics of fascism has taken mankind by surprise: ordinary people understand this political method as little as they would Riemann's geometry. But the point is that fascism denies even in theory the values that mankind has long taken for granted: everywhere respected. Because fascism has not even the check of hypocrisy, this system has been able to perpetrate infamies that, to less consistent exponents of evil, would hardly be conceivable.

One incident will provide an ultimate mark of fascist

debasement here. In its departure from any human value, it is worse than the strafing of innocent refugees; for torture and wholesale slaying have been the constant devices of barbarism in all ages. The last refinement in treason to humanity's hard-won efforts to be human took place in the invasion of Norway. The means was the use of Austrian troops who had learned the Norwegian language when, as babies and children during the terrible period of starvation at the end of the last war, they were taken in and nourished by kindly Norwegian families. That refinement of ingratitude reaches a depth of compact dirtiness well below the best previous records of fascism's debasement of the human soul.

In order to outwit this non-Euclidean politics, democracy must be prepared to play the human game with the same ruthless consistency that fascism plays the anti-human game. Tolerance must not mean tolerance of fascism's evils, and humanity must not mean leaning backward to do justice to the fascist victor in order to be sure that one is not unduly moved by sympathies for the victims. Peace belongs to men of good will; but against the violent, only a concentration of strength, as great as that which moves the fascist to his purposes, will suffice. There must be no quarter to those who mean ill and who, with deliberate maleficence, work ruin.

The notion that if one fights fascism one will become fascist has been one of the most popular aids to the spread of fascism. One might just as well say that an honest house-holder who confronts a burglar with a revolver will in turn become a burglar if he shoots. Indeed, a fascist must have invented that slippery phrase, and grinned in triumph when it went the rounds among democratic peoples who wanted an excuse for inaction.

The real truth is quite different: namely, that one cannot fight fascism without holding to a group of positive principles that are just as solid, just as consistent, just as determinedly used, as those that the fascist has employed. Our American democracy must have before its mind a coherent pattern of life, which will make sense to most democratic men; and to uphold that pattern it must be tough and ruthless, as ruthless as Sherman and as tough as Stonewall Jackson.

Unless our surviving democracies command a positive system of belief, hopes, loyalties—unless every member possesses this living faith—there is no chance of resisting fascism by any mere weight of armament, nor by any mere sweep of economic changes. For the purposes of aggression fascism has stopped at nothing: it has demanded dedications, abnegations, sacrifices, long in advance of actual battle and danger, greater than those men are usually willing to give except in moments of danger. Democracy must do the same. Unless democracy can summon up an equal spirit, it is lost.

That is why so far I have been examining the weaknesses in the philosophies and institutions that should have opposed fascism and that actually have miserably failed. Those weaknesses have been fatal. A fascist state built on wholly negative ethical principles is at least capable of action; ultimately destructive even of itself, perhaps, but temporarily successful. Such a state must be met by a faith and a force equally great. And to achieve that we must begin at the very beginning; not with armaments or loans; but with the beliefs for which men will gladly live, and if need be, gladly die.

PART FIVE:

The Recovery of Purpose

Without contraries is no progression. At-
traction and Repulsion, Reason and Energy,
Love and Hate, are necessary to Human
Existence.

. . . "More! More!" is the cry of a mistaken soul: less than All cannot satisfy Man.

WILLIAM BLAKE

The Recovery of Purpose

29. PROSPECTS FOR SURVIVAL

No matter how long the present war lasts or what its outcome may be, life will be difficult on this planet for another two generations: probably for at least another century. Until fascism is finally defeated there will be no peace for the peaceful, and no happy promise for the unborn. Recovery from this poisoned state will not come fast.

For millions of blasted men and women the best that life will offer will be meagre survival on a level hardly above animal existence. Their best sustenance in the dark hours will only be some remnant of hope for their children. Without that hope, without that possibility of biological renewal and spiritual re-birth, out of the depth of human love, the race would long ago have withered away. And no matter how strange may seem this stark wasteland we now confront, Man has walked here often before.

No fair weather philosophy will enable people to meet this condition. That is why counsels of optimism, counsels that rely with vulgar complacency upon things righting themselves in another thousand years, are the most debilitating and disheartening counsels of all. What are men and women to do before that time is up? After what has happened in Europe and Asia during the past decade no human being has a right to hope for automatic improvements or compensations.

Only the bitterest truth, the truth that human civilization is already almost lost, will be medicinal enough to save us. No sweet syrup can be added to that draught. Our very security has been undermined by those who believed, up to the last moment, that they might save themselves by glib promises and sordid compromises. These people even denied that any ideas or institutions threatened them, just as the benighted fools who governed England in 1936 denied that the Nazis were building airplanes in vast quantities.

What, then, are the prospects of survival? Can our Western civilization pass through the present crisis with even a handful of the scientific discoveries, the inventions, the literary and esthetic and scholarly achievements, the humanizing patterns of life that the last three centuries outlined? These were at least potential gifts and benefits to humanity; even if the mass of mankind had not yet fully participated in them.

If the answer to this question had to assume that the goods of modern civilization would be saved only on the condition that each person, each group, should go on behaving exactly as he or they behaved before fascism came into existence, the answer would be plain: survival is impossible. For Western society, in the form that it existed up to the present, was deeply corrupt. The cult of power was dominant in it; there were deep cleavages between class and class, race and race, nation and nation: it was mechanically unified and culturally disintegrated.

Probably we are now witnessing the last great crisis of this megalopolitan power civilization: with its centralized, overgrown cities, its slums and superslums, its drab and progressively meaningless routine based on a wholesale denial of the elemental needs and values of all living creatures, and an utter dearth of traditional roots and ideal aims. Parasitopolis—the city of parasites—no longer has the strength or will to defend itself; the passive barbarians within it will surrender to the active ones, unless they experience a swift transformation, which will bring back their morale. Tyrannopolis will reign over a ruined world unless—unless the disease creates the antidote.

As the crisis sharpens, as the evils that threaten us become more formidable, one possibility remains, born of the crisis itself: the psychological possibility of a large-scale conversion. Are our countrymen yet shattered enough to be ready for a re-integration: a change that will involve all our past routines and upset all our easy habits? Can our liberals sufficiently recover their faith to restore manfully the traditions of ideal liberalism? Will our sects and churches embrace that tradition of universalism which alone will guarantee human brotherhood in the days to come? Are they sufficiently capable of sacrifice to abandon the love of riches and power that cripples them? Will they take again to the catacombs rather than bow before Caesar? Will the separate nations guard what is left of their common birthright, lest they lose altogether their own?

These questions extend to every person and every group: for each of us has sinned and each of us has been weak; so each of us must be capable of repentance. Not one of us can escape reproach: not one of us but must undergo a profound change of heart and mind before he is fit to do his share in the work before us.

In this hour of need no petty measures will avail; no light renunciations are possible. The sphere of political action must rise above the limitations of the Economic Man; it must be as large as the fully developed personality, the fully developed community, large enough to conserve all the values of the past and to produce the seed of a more generous future than we in our time will ever enjoy.

No return to business as usual is possible; that day is past. No mere revamping of old economic programs, no revision of Marxism or extension of the New Deal, no mere ingenious political program, with a few socialistic planks added or taken away, no attempt to make five disparate economic systems produce profit in a community where new social motives must take the place of absent or dwindling profits—none of these shallow dodges will suffice.

192

We are being tested in fire and blood. Only a faith capable of passing through fire, only a sacrifice of blood, with complete indifference to our individual safety or our petty fortunes, will guarantee the survival of humanity itself at a level above that of a sub-human barbarism.

During the last three centuries Western society produced a worldwide fabric of thought and practical co-operation on almost every plane. Lack of moral direction, perversity of class and national interests, a deep-seated ideological decay, undermined this society and threw it open to barbarism at the very moment when it felt most confident of the onward sweep of science and invention. Within a short span of years—thanks to the deliberate ferocity with which the fascists have exterminated scholars and scientists—science and technics will all but disappear from Europe. In America the pace of technics will appreciably slacken, even should we have the luck to escape; for more than a billion men, more or less free, were needed to produce the culture we shared.

If the barbarians conquer Europe and therewith the African, Asiatic, and South American outposts, the outlook is far worse. This will mean that all our energies will be drawn off in the Herculean task of getting ready for war—and fighting it. We may preserve our traditions and our liberties; but the cost will be a heavy one.

We surely cannot accomplish the feat of preserving the Western Hemisphere for free government and for a civilized way of life in any spirit of prudence or carefully measured sacrifice. We must give ourselves utterly to the task, risking all in order that we may save the essence of our humanity. This means that we must be ready, not merely to fight at the drop of the hat, but to take under the protection of our free institutions countries that Nazism is ready to pounce on, before Nazism has a chance to act.

No military arm sufficient only to defend our own borders from a presumably distant enemy is strong enough to perform the tasks we must demand of ourselves. We need an overwhelming force, ready to strike on behalf of liberty and democracy and justice with overwhelming audacity: ready, like the armies of Napoleon, to *impose* liberty and democracy if need be rather than to see them perish utterly from the earth. Democracy must dare. To stand still in a world threatened by the demonic energies fascism has let loose is to go backward—into slavery itself. Our comrades and our allies unto death are all other civilized, freedom-loving men, whether they live in Greenland or Patagonia, in Great Britain and Ireland or in China and India.

In short, the crisis we face now demands a complete and wholehearted dedication to the prime ends of life: a dedication as complete as that which Great Britain made in form when, faced with the disasters of Flanders, it turned itself, for duration of the war, into a totalitarian democracy. The totalitarian element will be inescapable:

that is war. No part of our existence will go untouched.

But the democracy is also real; for the purpose that must be safeguarded at every step is the right of free citizens to exercise rational choice and decision, to live under a system of law instead of a personal despotism, to freely choose or reject their governors, and to make both their political and their economic institutions conform to their physical, their social, and their moral needs.

To achieve this large-scale sacrifice, to summon up such heroic energies, two further measures are necessary. First, we must erect a common goal of living, sufficient to stir the young out of their lethargy and cynicism and to give new meaning to every life in our democracy. And along with this must go a readiness to scrap swiftly every institutional arrangement, every habit of thought and action, that does not contribute either to the safety of our country, or to the intensification and enlargement of human life. Ideal values come first: we must make men and women before we make machines; and the esthetic and moral quality of their lives will be the very test of our mastery of machines.

What is demanded, as the very basis of our effort to preserve civilization, is a re-birth of the positive values of life. We must come to a fresh understanding of the basic issues of good and evil, power and form, force and grace, freedom and discipline in the actual world. "Less than all," I repeat, "cannot satisfy Man."

The crisis, then, presses toward a conversion, deepseated, organic, religious in essence, so that no part of political or personal existence will be untouched by it. This is the optimism of pathology. Out of corruption, health; out of weakness, salvation. We can have hope today precisely because the situation is absolutely desperate, because it demands of us the impossible—namely, that which would not be possible in an easier situation, which gave us some hope of wriggling out on lighter terms.

Such a conversion is needed if we are to rise above the shallow, desiccated pragmatism that served as a substitute for religion, and that money-centered economy which served as a substitute for dear life. Only the living— those for whom life has meaning—can continue to live and willingly make the fierce sacrifices that the present moment demands. All others are fascist slave-fodder—or are already dead. Living, for all of us, will be a long, desperate fight: a fight against anti-social states, organizing terror and slaughter on a planetary scale; a fight, in any event, to recover for our children and grandchildren the essentials of a human life. Whitman has uttered the words that should be on our lips as we face this future:

Revolt! and the bullet for tyrants!
Did we think victory great?
So it is—But now it seems to me, when it cannot be help'd,
    that defeat is great,
And that death and dismay are great.

196

30. FRAMEWORK OF FAITH

Faith for living touches levels at which speech is impossible. One's life must demonstrate that for which one truly lives. The best cannot be told; the best is that which must always be left untold. But if we are to think decisively, act cleanly, unite as a nation and as a member of a group of nations into a purposive life, the first step is our philosophic reorientation.

Until we establish a central core of purpose, all lesser practical proposals must be lacking in force and driving power, indeed, in significance; for their meaning derives as much from their ideal context as from their social application. To understand this one need look no further than fascism itself. What distinguishes the followers of Hitler and Mussolini are not their resources, for Germany and Italy are relatively weak; and not their technological facility, for in many departments they were inferior to England and France.

What distinguishes these fascist nations is their metaphysical purpose. Humanly repulsive, hostile to love and reason: yes. But a purpose: a collective ideal that embodied itself in a concrete program. The strength of fascism is that, with whatever violence and outrage to the

197

spirit of intelligent human co-operation, it made institutions and material necessities the agents of human will. If fascists can do this, rational human beings cannot do less. Reason would be worse than futile if it led to a meek acceptance of social paralysis.

The base of a new life must be a system of values. Where are these to be found? One thing is sure: one may no longer, like the old-fashioned economic reformers or socialists, seek these values in the existing economic system, or imagine that if we have a hundred horsepower car, we will automatically be provided with a map, a guide, and a knowledge of what city we are aiming at.

Most of the ethical philosophies of the past, however, have sought to isolate the goods of life and to make one or another of them supreme. They have looked upon pleasure or efficiency or sacrifice or imperturbability or self-annihilation as the chief end of a disciplined and cultivated spirit, and as the crown of life in society. Since no one goes through the world unhurt, since all shoot but few hit the mark, since violence and injustice often have the upper hand, these earlier systems sought by a kind of moral bookkeeping to redress the evils of earthly existence: so much debited here, so much added in Heaven—a promissory note, a non-negotiable draft, to make up for a shortage of funds in actual life.

To seek pleasure or happiness or length of days has been the common goal of all these traditional faiths—if not now, then hereafter. But though ideal ends are, as I have shown, indispensable for guiding practical conduct, no single set of ends suffices to cover human existence. The fact that sunshine is beneficial to the body in reasonable amounts does not make the Sahara an attractive place to live in. If no single principle will produce an harmonious and well-balanced life, for either the personality or the community, then harmony and balance are perhaps the essential ends for which we must provide.

Now values emerge in actual life at all its levels. There is virtue as Plato saw in the good shoemaker who produces an honest pair of shoes no less than in the philosopher whose life is dedicated to the pursuit of abstract truth. Science is good, but not good for love. Love is good, but not good for mechanical invention. Mechanical inventions are good, but no good for transcribing into esthetic symbols the feelings and perceptions of the painter, which are expressible only through a delicate unison of hand, eye, and pigment, which thus record layers and layers of accumulated experience, his own and that of countless predecessors.

Every good, then, is organically conditioned by other goods. Hence the wise Biblical injunction: "Be not virtuous over-much; why shouldst thou destroy thyself?" And so play, which may be quite ruinous to professional athletes and turn them into useless dullards, may be the salvation of a hard-paced executive or a scientist steeped

199

in laboratory research. It is in the organic pattern of a life in society, a life in space and time, a life that is communal no less than personal, that each good reveals itself.

We cannot, then, build our values upon any single abstract end; for these abstractions themselves have meaning and power only in relation to the unity of human experience. This unity is not a temporary state, not the work of a generation; it is the composite product of all that man has achieved, all that he is, all that he hopes to be, so far as finite minds, with limited powers of observation and a limited record of history, can grasp. In confronting human history, however, nothing is more plain than the presence and persistence of the ideal. This distinguishes humanity from brute creation as plainly as feathered wings and the capacity for flight distinguishes birds from all other vertebrates.

Where are the foundations for these ideals: in external nature? On the contrary, man is born into a world of human values and human associations. He knows life from the beginning, not as a fact in the raw, but only as he makes use of the society about him and uses the tools and instruments and modes of expression that society has developed and conserved. Words, gestures, abstract symbols of number, grammar, logic come to him first, though of course without these labels: they come naturally through human intercourse, as the member of a family—or a human substitute for the family. After that, in good time, science, religion, philosophy, art.

From birth on, in other words, man finds himself living primarily in a world of values and purposes. Some of these are partly ingrained in our animal nature, like the sense of family loyalty, but even in the earliest phases, even in the most primitive manifestations, they are re-inforced and re-validated by social usages.

The essential forms of communion and communication are already present in the relation of the mother to her baby: this is a prelude to wider fellowships, if not deeper understandings. From the mother's mouth comes the great-est of all gifts to the personality, articulate speech, out of which thought flows, through channels long cut by tribes whose very name has vanished. The rationalists of the eighteenth century, like La Mettrie, likened the world to a machine; but human experience tells another story: In the beginning was the Word. By means of the word, man has translated a world of confused feelings, sensations, motor activities, into a world of meanings.

In short, man's greatest triumph in producing order out of chaos, greater than law, greater than science, was lan-guage. To keep the channels of human communication clean is a duty as primal—and holy—as guarding the sacred fire was for primitive man. He who debases the word, as the fascists have so unsparingly done, breeds darkness and confusion and all manner of foulness.

201

Life begins with symbols and values that derive, not from immediate experience, but from a long human heritage which men have labored to keep alive through many a time of troubles. These values emerge concretely in the affections of the family groups; in the words of greeting and kindness and delight that gradually shade over into more deliberate, more subtle efforts at communion, or feeling together, and communication, or thinking together.

Only by a long process of discipline has man disentangled himself from this world of values sufficiently to see—as a result of this deliberate abstraction—that he also lives in what he calls a physical universe. In experience, that universe is secondary; and indeed the most patient see and touch only a small part of it. Most human experience is by the method of sampling; it is through our values and symbols that we grasp the underlying connections.

The failure to understand the simple natural history of values and things has caused people to give to the physical universe and its understanding the first place in their scheme. But in actuality, one begins with the complete tissue of human experience, in the midst of a family group and a social order that is already a going concern. Only by a deliberate sloughing off of one's central human interests can one reach "the physical universe." In experience, the social arts take precedence, not only of the social sciences, but of the physical arts of using fire and tools

202

and machines to modify the environment and make man—
the purpose is revealing—more at home.

This orientation is important. If it is correct, values are
not added to a world that exists independently without
values: on the contrary, that seemingly independent world
was finally abstracted, after centuries of patient study,
from the world of values, a world of impulse and purpose
and life, in which man primarily lives. Values are not
cemented on to the ugly structure of physical existence as
in a bad piece of architecture, without affecting either the
function or the design. Values are, on the contrary, present
from the very beginning. This is true historically of the
development of all culture; and it is true in the development of the human personality within a particular culture.

Not alone are values present in all human experience,
even when concealed or neglected: they exercise a determining influence in the choice of abstractions and in the
use of power. Speaking mathematically, the sign of value
is as important in every human situation as the sign of
quantity. How much? is the question of science. But how
good? how significant? and how beautiful? are no less
critical. This is true in every area of behavior, not merely
in what one calls moral conduct.

Whether the physical universe itself, now that we have
opened it up and staked it out, implies life and value is a
still unsolved question. A century ago the possibility was
vigorously denied by many scientists, but the highly orig-

inal reasoning of a philosophic bio-chemist, Lawrence Henderson, gives us now far more reason for holding that the cosmos is itself life-directed than once seemed possible. The vague stir within us, which we associated with the beat of our hearts and the expansion of our lungs, seems to require for continued sustenance a whole solar system, merely to maintain such elementary relations as the heat of our blood.

Sleeping or waking, we keep in rhythm with our brother, the Sun, even though we boast a little too loudly of our power of turning night into day. So, despite our air-conditioned houses, the first return of spring for an inhabitant of the Northern zones quickens the pulse almost as much as it did the cowering cave-dweller's. The more thoroughly we explore the universe with telescope and microscope, with crucible, test-tube, and thermometer, the more wonderful become the rhymes and correspondences that bind man not only to the animal orders from which he has emerged, but to the farthest galaxies of the heavens—and the more do our symbols themselves fall into harmonious order, with symmetries and correspondences like that of the periodic table.

When one contemplates the marvelous Being which encloses us, one acquires a deeper respect for all those cultural resources which have made the very act of contemplation possible. At such moments we behold in our own divinity the promise of a greater one that man can never come face to face with: the purpose that bottoms all purposes: the perfection that surpasses all perfections.

But we approach nature through the medium of our human culture; there is no other means of access. All that we have and know and believe is the result of those personal values whose long conservation has made it possible for us to explore, at very last, an impersonal world. Here by a superb act of thoughtful abnegation, man has —for the purpose of clear vision—displaced his own values, his own feelings and interests. But the values come first: the true word, the right deed, the beautiful gesture, the polite act—all that, growing out of the family, makes human life possible, even among strangers, even among those who, separated by distance, are on their honor to observe even stricter standards of truth and righteousness.

Patiently accumulated, these values are nevertheless recurrently lost: they are prey to fire, earthquake or war, which ruin the frail physical structures that embody them; but they leave their mark, even when defaced, on the minds of men: a fragment of Sappho or Sophocles, a mutilated torso from the hand of Praxiteles, renews men's confidence in life itself. When no other means are left, parents tell their children, and the old the young. In this work of transmission even the poor and the oppressed and the humble have played their part.

All our values are both personal and communal; who shall say where one begins and the other leaves off? Indi-

vidualism, therefore, in the sense of isolation, is merely
a spatial illusion. The more self-sufficient an individual
seems to be, the more sure it is that, like Thoreau at Wal-
den Pond, he carries a whole society within his bosom.

Only in the most dire extremity of being lost or deserted
does the individual have the burden of existing for a short
time by his solitary endeavors. When that happens, as it
may to a man lost in the woods or forced down with his
plane in the desert, the very impulse that keeps him alive
is the desire to return to his family or fellows: the image
of his wife, or child, or friend, is what spurs him to undertake the superhuman efforts that may be necessary for
survival. Woe to him if he must depend upon water and
food alone to keep going!

Even the walled-in hermit of the Middle Ages, alone
with his mortifications and his God, relied upon the
charitable help of his fellow villagers for at least bread
and water. Isolation from society brings death just as
surely as physical starvation. And there are degrees of
this death: enmity, truculence, ignorance, apathy, uncom-
municativeness, lying, non-co-operation are some of its
modes: modes deeply fatal to mind and body. These
acts of isolation, once assumed in defiance of society,
must sometimes be applied for the protection of society
to those who choose to deny the social bond. The community must isolate the criminal and the insane, not in
punishment, but in the effort to curb further disintegra-

tion. Hence the prison and asylum: hence war against collective criminality.

As in so many other cases, this analysis holds as true for whole communities as for persons. Both physically and spiritually we are members one of another. That is not a new discovery and it does not depend alone upon the facts of modern technology; for we have never been otherwise. It is only callous pride and ignorance and egoism that have sometimes made men insensitive to their true condition and estate.

31. CREATING AND SHARING VALUES

Man's chief purpose, then, is the creation and preservation of values: that is what gives meaning to our civilization, and the participation in this is what gives significance, ultimately, to the individual human life.

Only in so far as values are fostered—through art and religion and science and love and domestic life—can men effectively use the machines and powers that have enabled them to tame nature and secure human existence from the worst outrages and accidents that forever threaten it. Civilization, our very capacity to be human, rests on that perpetual effort. If any nation or group thinks that the job is finished, or if man puts his confidence solely in the instruments and forgets the ends and ideals and metaphysical purposes—then the structure crumbles away: then man himself is finished.

Thought, social relations, economic practices, biological activities, cosmic backgrounds—all these are organically united and call for co-operations that reach out beyond the borders of any single community, even as they reach out, beyond our limited present, into the past and future. That which exists by itself has, indeed, no real existence at all; it is a phantasm, an aberration of the mind.

The finer life becomes, the more complicated becomes the network of relationships, and the more invisible filaments bind part with part.

Goethe once put this truth admirably in a conversation with Eckermann. "People," he said, "are always talking about originality; but what do they mean? As soon as we are born, the world begins to work upon us, and keeps on to the end. What can we call ours except energy, strength, will? If I could give an account of what I owe to great predecessors and contemporaries, there would be but a small remainder." That does not merely hold for Goethe; it holds for every human group, every community, every person.

The individual who fancies he has made his own professional career, or the inventor who believes he has the sole right to his invention, or the business man who thinks his own unaided efforts have brought him his fortune is merely ignorant of his debts. Like Bounderby, whom Dickens portrayed in "Hard Times," he is a monster of ingratitude. Darwin formulated his "Origin of Species" with the sense that he was making a completely unique personal discovery. Before he was finished the similar hypothesis of another young naturalist, Wallace, was brought to his attention: it turned out that they had both got their clue from Malthus's "Essay on Population." By the time Darwin published his second edition, he had at last become aware of a whole line of predecessors and partial anticipators, extending back to the Greeks.

209

The individual contribution, the work of any single generation, is infinitesimal: the power and glory belong to human society at large, and are the long result of selection, conservation, sacrifice, creation, and renewal—the outcome of endless brave efforts to conserve values and ideas, and to hand them on to posterity, along with physical life itself. Each person is a temporary focus of forces, vitalities, and values that carry back into an immemorial past and that reach forward into an unthinkable future. The best consolation for the dying is the thought that others, equally good, will carry on their work: that is the comfort the father and mother derive from their children, that the teacher derives from his student, that comrades and colleagues pass on to each other.

Men are individually nothing except in relation to that greater reality, Man. And Man himself is nought except in relation to that greater reality which he calls divine. Thought, art, love are all intimations of this divinity: flickerings of man-made filaments that connect, in our imaginations, with distant flashes in the dark impenetrable sky.

This, then, is the philosophic justification for every form of social justice: not merely for a sharing of material goods and animal satisfactions, sufficient to sustain life on its humblest levels—though this is important—but also for that degree of cultivation and leisure which makes possible a fuller sharing of all the higher goods of life.

In America we have an historic tradition that recognizes both needs. The Land Grant act that was passed during the Civil War was an attempt to give to every able and willing family that would stake out a homestead a generous share in the land of our Republic. In another period of crisis, the distribution of work by the W.P.A. was a recognition of the same principle. Embedded still deeper in our traditions is the free elementary school education, now extending even through high school and college, which we have taken to be the inalienable right of every member of the community; as a very means of ensuring his fitness to be an intelligent and responsible member of that community.

Within very definite limits, differentiation of talent must be recognized and differentiation of reward may be serviceable; but never to such an extent as to continue the gross inequalities, the grotesque specialisms, the unpardonable parasitisms that have grown up in the United States—as in the whole Western World—during the past century.

Differentiated tasks, individual preferences, special incentives, intense interests, must all be taken into account in allowing for the full growth of the human personality. But this can happen with justice only after the continuity and security of the person and the community itself are secured. Every attempt to depart from the rule of justice, and to put first, not that which all men must have, but that which a few are able to seize, must defeat the permanent

211

interests of human society. When justice is flouted, in order to give precedence to large holders of capital or landed property, to create a fixed caste with special privileges, or to preserve property itself without respect for its social functions and its duties to the whole community, the result is an evil one. It often ends in the very downfall of the protected caste, through inanition, failure of nerve, sheer laziness.

The first move in the direction of justice is to remove, by example, the false scheme of values that has so long prevailed in Western society. Bread and circuses are no substitute for justice: they lower both the giver and the receiver. Profits and power and special privilege cannot remain as the main motive force of a society that seeks to preserve democratic values and personal liberties: for it is ultimately the one-sided concern with these values that has vitiated and corrupted and now desperately endangered our whole civilization.

The fundamental values of a true community are elsewhere: in love, poetry, disinterested thought, the free use of the imagination, the pursuit of non-utilitarian activities, the production of non-profitmaking goods, the enjoyment of non-consumable wealth—here are the sustaining values of a living culture. To be alive is to hear, to see, to feel, to touch, to shape, to manipulate, to think, and create: then to intensify all these experiences through an organized system of recording and preserving and reproducing them, through the church and the art museum and the concert hall and the laboratory and the school. This is the headwater and reservoir of social life: the Grand Coulee Dam of our whole culture which will finally create a lake from which energy and life will flow into even the most arid spots of human existence.

A community whose life is not irrigated by art and science, by religion and philosophy, day upon day, is a community that exists half alive. A personality who has not entered into this realm has not yet reached the human estate. The very means and instruments of daily routine, our houses and our clothes, our motor cars and our factories, are conditioned by the existence of these other needs that spring out of the needs of the personality: otherwise those who use them are barbarians—or robots— or at best children playing vacantly with toys.

By the same token, these physical structures are stripped of their *proper* significance *as means* when they are condemned to serve as substitutes for life itself. The finest phonograph in the world is no substitute for the hum of a happy mother bending over her child. The most satiny Hollywood boudoir never can make up for the lack of a passionate lover. The most expensive costume will not, when the body must come into play, atone for its limp irresponsiveness; just as the most luxurious student dormitories will never serve the cause of education as well as the presence of intelligent and courageous professors.

213

Life must not wait on physical paraphernalia. Life must come first. "The pretty country folk who lie between the acres of the rye, with a heigh, and a ho, and a hey-nonny-no" may well laugh at the Hollywood boudoir.

Our economic activities, during the era that boasted so loudly of industrial progress, failed to achieve their full potentialities for life. This was in no small part because the goods that the machine could produce so plentifully were not justly shared. Hence poverty, secondary starvation, crime, theft, sordid and battered environments, occupied by depressed and battered people: the industrial environment of the larger part of Western civilization.

Our society was divided against itself. It sought progress and it found itself faced with a dead end: economic crises and wars. It boasted of wealth, and its vast mass of tenant farmers, unemployed workers and underfed children proclaimed its poverty. So we had dearth in the midst of plenty, war in the midst of peace, riches atop of squalor, and, finally, a growing wave of irrationality and superstition and man-worship in a period when exact scientific research had even entered industry.

Human culture, plainly, cannot be sustained unless values enter into every activity. Otherwise we are cursed with a Sunday morality, in which decency and brotherhood and justice are flouted for six days and then piously reinstated on the seventh: a system under which our deeds never by any accident coincide with our professions.

214

The Athenians were right in believing that the ultimate goods of life could be enjoyed only by free men; they meant by this that they can not be fully enjoyed if they are offered to people who are forced to spend their days in some spiritually deadening or physically exhausting task, whether in the market, the mine, or the workshop. Human development requires both periods of activity and periods of leisure, in which the results of this activity may be meditated upon, absorbed, digested. One of the reasons that country folk, with limited experience, are nevertheless so much better companions for an artist or a thinker than city people of the same class, is that the former have always kept for themselves a little free time to sit still and brood, whittling wood around a winter fire, or bent impassively over a fishing pole, watching the trout's canny flirtations. The city worker may be better read; but the countryman is more reflective: such experience as he has encountered he has salted down.

But it is equally true—and the intellectual tends always to forget this—that spiritual life suffers by complete divorce from the vivid experiences and the salutary restraints of practical activity. The Athenians, fortunately, before they became engrossed in imperialist ambitions, managed to retain in some measure their hold upon the fundamental manual and operative realities of sport and war. They had tough muscles and well-tempered bodies and eyes quick to note how the grapes were ripening or how the potter molded his clay on the wheel. That sense distinguished Plato from every philosopher down to Descartes. So it is possibly no accident that the most original mind among the Athenians was a stone-cutter by trade and the son of a midwife, or that perhaps the greatest tragic dramatist was also a general. Nor was it an accident, in our own American Golden Day, that Henry Thoreau was a pencil maker and a surveyor, that Herman Melville was a sailor, that Walt Whitman was a carpenter and a printer good enough to set up his own "Leaves of Grass"; or that Abe Lincoln was a rail-splitter who retained to the end of his life a solid confidence in himself that was based on his sure axmanship and shoulders that could carry a heavier burden than his neighbor's.

The segregation of the spiritual life from the practical life is a curse that falls impartially upon both sides of our existence. A society that gives to one class all the opportunities for leisure, and to another all the burdens of work, dooms both classes to spiritual sterility. The first will make busy work for itself: games, fox hunts, parties, organized inanities; while the other will make work itself empty, and even go the forces that make it empty one better, by reducing work to "as little as you can get away with"— only to lose self-respect as well as craftsmanlike pleasure in that very act. One of the main tasks of a purposive intelligence is to keep the inner world and the outer, the spiritual and the practical, the personal and the mechanical

216

or automatic, in constant interaction. They form a dynamic unity.

The moral to be drawn from this is that servile labor—even if it produces social necessities—should be minimized to the utmost. The problem is not entirely solved by the invention of automatic machines; because, if pushed too far, the routine of mechanized production robs those engaged in it, and even more those displaced by it, of the opportunities for educative, person-satisfying activities. Such work as remains servile or dangerous in our society—whether on the assembly line or on the battlefield—should be shared by the entire adult community.

In short, justice demands either equality of life-sustenance and leisure, in times of plenty and peace, or equality of sacrifice in times of hardship and war. The principle is the same in both cases; and if we introduce the element of sacrifice into our economic system now, where it will affect principally the middle classes and those above them, we may as a country have some guarantee for fruitful and refined leisure—for the good life itself—when at long last we emerge from this murky period.

32. LIFE IS BETTER THAN UTOPIA

Economic justice would extend to the whole community the decent practices of the human household. It would share food and shelter and all that is needful for life with the young and the old and the infirm, who cannot work, as well as with the unemployed who are temporarily withdrawn from work. All other forms of reward must wait upon this general sharing; it is a first claim on all agriculture and industry. No other system makes sense.

The more automatic machines become, the more consistently workers are thrown out of industry, the more absurd it is to make the goods of life come solely as a reward for labor. Universal service: private service or public service—that, and not the actual hours or days of work performed, should be the key to economic reward. The artist or the scientist does not ask for an eight-hour day; he wishes that nature would grant him a twenty-four-hour day, and thereby intensify his happiness. But by the same token, one who is employed only two hours a day requires as much food and drink and shelter, roughly, as if he were working ten hours. Readiness for service should be the chief condition for the active worker's reward.

If the free peoples of the world should achieve peace

218

within another generation, and produce once more a surplus that need not go into armament, then the principle of reward is plain: social responsibility and service for all, high standards of work and co-operative effort—and then a social dividend in goods and leisure for all. The food stamp disposal of agricultural surpluses to families on the W.P.A. rolls is a crude indication of a method that has far wider application in a rational society. Never again must we burn, destroy, or withhold that for which men have need.

But though these principles are important for a just community one cannot therefore hold, with an older school of revolutionary thinkers, that the evils of life are entirely the work of an ominous exploiting class, or that they are entirely economic in origin, and would disappear from life entirely under a more humane regime. It is this exorbitant belief in middle-class comforts—and in what money can buy—that has persistently betrayed the working classes themselves in their efforts to challenge the existing holders of power and improve their position. They did not ask for justice and freedom; they did not ask for responsible copartnership; they asked, in the main, for just a little more of the gravy. Even then they asked for this, not on behalf of the working class, but on behalf of a special group—the Union of Flypaper Stickers, or the Brotherhood of Doughnut-hole Drillers. Their standards, alas! were almost as low as those of their opponents.

The notion that mechanical invention and increased wealth would finally do away with all the evils of life is as untrue to human experience as the notion that salvation lies wholly and fully within the individual soul. Real life is far better than the Sunday School utopias that satisfied the nineteenth century. And this is precisely because real life is, from the standpoint of the smug advocates of progress, incurably worse: dogged forever by radical evil.

Among the progressive and liberal thinkers of the last century, there was scarcely one who did not assume that mankind either was permanently good, or might sooner or later reach such a state of universal beatitude. They thought that, with good economic and political arrangements, life might become a long picnic on a sunny summer afternoon, a picnic in a world from which even the mosquitoes might, with a vigilant Public Health Service, be kept away. *"A nous, à nous la liberté!"*

Even Karl Marx, terrible realist that he was, shared this sweet dogma. Did he not renounce his own theory of the dialectics of change, and proclaim that a time might come when the state would wither away, and a classless society, without oppositions, without conflicts, without any sort of social insufficiency or evil, would come into existence. In short: pie in the sky by-and-by!

But though the human personality seeks perfection, its salvation lies in the effort, not in the actual achievement. Perfection itself would mean death. Man cannot live for long on distilled water alone; he needs organic food, which would be useless to him were it not, by its nature, subject to decomposition and decay. William James knew this when he escaped from the middle-class paradise of mediocre thoughts and amiable dispositions that was called Chautauqua.

Those who think that evil can be permanently abolished always feel grossly betrayed when they find it has come back again: they are like the heroine in the old-fashioned village melodrama whose innocence permits her to be seduced in every act. They diligently root the weed out of the next field, these guileless ones, only to find that while their back was turned it has started growing in their own garden.

This belief in being permanently able to dispose of evil is a childish one. It exhibits, as it were, an unfathomable shallowness. Part of the vicious disappointment that people suffered from at the end of the first World War was due to their immodest expectations of human goodness: they hoped too fervently, and then, taking revenge, they despaired too blackly, and became limp with melancholy, dissolute with disillusion.

We Americans were particularly to blame in this respect. We sacrificed astronomical sums of money, and not a few lives to save democracy. Having done this, we expected that at the end of that fierce and rancorous conflict, in which other men had been engaged for four searing

221

years, the beat of angels' wings would at once be heard in the sky and concord and brotherly love would immediately settle over the earth. That lack of realism was fatal to us: that too-virtuous idealism, that too exacting purity, is even now taking its toll in cynical inertia.

Our actions were sound when we went into the first World War; but our dreams were vain ones; for they were founded on the belief that one single high act would enable us to live happily ever afterward, without further duties, further burdens. A childish dream indeed: all the worse because it was dreamed by cool-headed rationalists and not revivalist preachers. The latter might with better reason have fancied that they could turn the world into a huge revival meeting, full of repentant sinners and overnight saints. It is a tough day for "idealists" when they finally learn that there are no permanent victories. At that point, they either become useful men or turn into resentful neurotics.

One must guard against such overwrought expectations: they do injustice to our very humanity. Faith for living means being able to go on stoutly in a world where even the closest lovers quarrel and true friends misunderstand one another. We must recognize that it is fantastic to think that we can establish a perfect justice, which will call for no further remedies, or discover a perfect truth, which will call for no corrections. It is even more puerile, if that were possible, to believe that once we get the mechanism properly adjusted, creating full employment in the factory or balancing the endocrines in the human personality, the community will remain in that utterly blissful state. This is the error that has been made by those who have worshiped the American Constitution so heartily that they have resisted every effort to make it produce freedom and democracy for a quite different kind of economic society.

But more than this: the effort to achieve a permanent state of bliss would be self-negating. Evil and good are phases in the process of educative growth; and who shall say which is the better teacher? Illness, error, defeat, frustration, disintegration, malicious accident—all these elements are as much in the go of life as waste, nutrition, and repair.

In other words, the very forces which, if triumphant, would utterly destroy life are needful to season experience and deepen understanding. Even virtue, as Samuel Butler said, must be mixed with a little of its opposite. That is why the higher religions cannot dispense with symbols for this fact: Ahriman, Kali, Satan. These destroyers, too, are in some sense at the service of life. Without these antagonists, human life would be merely a pageant passing before the eyes of bored spectators, not a high drama that awakens exaltation by pity and terror.

Those who aim at goodness are often carried to their destination by the very road they consciously seek to avoid: for it is not the absence of temptation, nor the failure to sin, that turns a weak person into a saint. In achieving a life abundant success lies, not in escaping evil, as a Brahman avoids taking life by having even the insects swept out of his path, but by turning negative forces to the account of the personality itself.

Observing the large place of evil, the high religions have celebrated almost solely the negative aspects of existence. They have confronted death and extinction in all their forms; and have been concerned above all with the relief of the ailing and the salvation of the transgressor. In the early Christian Church this preoccupation often reached the point of downright morbidity. Some of the early Fathers talked as if no one should have a child because babies get ill, cause their parents endless anxiety, and sometimes die early; or grow up and come to no good end. So it was again in the Reformation and Counter-Reformation: the religious minds tended to deny all positive joys and delights, and, forever putting up their umbrellas to keep off the storm, they never enjoyed the moments of sunshine.

In reactions against this one-sided pessimism, the optimistic rationalists of the nineteenth century, and their successors today, have committed the opposite extravagance: they have been in search of the land of perpetual sunshine. Because of their unrealistic assumptions these people have not merely ignored the positive and compensatory role of evil in the human economy; they have also overlooked the fact that the parts of good and evil are often reversed. That is to say, the goods of life have themselves a large capacity for mischief. Who has not observed the charity that poisoned the giver, and the brotherhood that is based on hatred for the outsider? In fact, nothing needs such constant watching and revision as the practice of the virtues. Before one realizes it, as Emerson pointed out in "Uriel," goods become evils, just as pacifism has become one of the chief abettors of brutal aggression in the present world.

But similarly, the evils of life have a certain capacity for good: an adultery may sometimes cement a marriage rather than destroy it, and the destruction of hearing or the loss of a limb may grant new powers to other organs and new perspectives to the mind of the person afflicted. The mature person knows that evils must be faced, embraced, assimilated. He knows that to shun them or innocently hope to eliminate them forever is to cling to an existence that is both false to reality and lacking in definition and in depth.

Like arsenic, evil is a tonic in grains and a poison in ounces. The real problem of evil—the problem that justifies every attempt to sublimate war into legal conflict, to abolish economic poverty, and to cure disease—is to reduce evil to amounts that can be spiritually assimilated.

This doctrine is plainly just the opposite of the life-denying habits of mind which have become widely popular during the last century: particularly the notion that comfort, safety, the absence of physical disease and the postponement of death, are the ultimate blessings of civilization; that as these blessings spread, the evils of life will be automatically abolished. The fallacy of this view lies in the fact that comfort and safety and length of life are not absolute goods. On the contrary: they are capable of defeating life just as much as hardship and disease and uncertainty. The belief that man's more essential needs must be subordinated to the production of increasing amounts of comforts and luxuries—motor cars and air-conditioned houses and tricky cigarette-lighters and endless supplies of cosmetics and anesthetics—is a dark superstition. This is the heresy of a society corrupted by love of money and by spiritual emptiness. No wonder the great artists and philosophers of the last century, from Ruskin to Tolstoy, from Delacroix to Daumier, from Emerson to Nietzsche, revolted against that society and rejected all its values. They cast out the religion of comfort as fiercely as Francis of Assisi would have cast it out.

By accepting this heresy as the essential modern creed the so-called party of progress has in fact been a party of reaction: that is to say, it has reacted against the more central needs of human life itself. As a result, our American community has been oriented to things. It has every sort of possession except self-possession, and every sort of security except a social order founded on the essential nature of man: above all, his capacity for love and sacrifice.

By putting business before every other manifestation of life, our apostles of the machine have forgotten the chief business of life, namely, growth, reproduction, development, creation. They have paid infinite attention to perfecting the mechanism of the incubator—and have forgotten the egg. Hence the practical men have turned out to be the most cobwebby Utopians. Meanwhile, real life is better than their wildest dreams: for the world of personality embraces evil as well as good, and by that act, it transcends the worst mischiefs and destructions that life presents.

Only by recognizing these truths can one face the totality of human experience and take the bad weather along with the good. This is an obvious statement, perhaps, in moments of crisis; but it is one that must be borne in mind, incorporated into all our plans and expectations. Evil must be continually confronted, continually be *lived down*. The good and the bad are forever in a deadly grapple; and there is no referee who will break them in a clinch. Proteus-like, good and evil change their nature in the very act of combat: hence the need for doubled watchfulness in living; hence the virtuous must guard against their own virtue!

In sum: life is not Utopia. But it is life, and that is better than Utopia. Even in its most catastrophic and disconcerting moments, life brings high gifts to the living. Lovers are often closest at the moment of parting; and no man suspects his strength until in a desperate moment he summons his scattered powers together, and, fighting every inch of the way to the grave, he outwits his most stubborn enemy, death.

PART SIX:

Personal Development: Social Renewal

Listen! I will be honest with you;
I do not offer the old smooth prizes,
    but offer rough new prizes;
These are the days that must happen to
    you. . . .

WALT WHITMAN

PART SIX

Personal Development and Social Renewal

33. THE NEEDS OF THE LIVING

Faith for living needs rational statement; so that which is mutely felt may be shared and understood. I have tried to frame this statement in terms of the real nature of personality and community. It follows, if my reasoning is correct, that the intelligent and proper use of the machine, of political organizations, or of natural resources does not by itself guarantee this faith. Just the opposite is true. It is because man inherits, through long historic effort, a world of values that all his instrumental material activities have reason and meaning—or, as we say, make sense.

No doubt it is well, the author of "Democratic Vistas" reminds us, to act *as if* these material things by themselves were real; as if they had an independent existence. But without the support of human values and purposes our great bridges will become rusting masses of twisted steel, and our huge hydro-electric turbines will continue to deliver power to factories too bare of life to tempt a nest of rats. Unless we rebuild values our activities, no matter how rationalized and refined, or however impregnated with science, will remain insensate: that is, dull, blind, unresponsive to the needs of personality.

231

But now comes the next question: how is this faith to be embodied? What old interests must be restored; what new fields of activity staked out? How, in other words, are we to achieve fresh energies for living precisely at the moment when our lives are threatened, and our whole society is overwhelmed by the necessity to subdue violence, curb destruction, and restore the very possibilities of human existence to millions that are now harried, maimed, starving, homeless, enslaved?

These questions become all the more important because so many of the tasks imposed on us are of their nature brutal and soul-deadening ones. To meet the military powers of fascism we must ourselves create a superior military power; indeed we must not merely match blow for blow and plane for plane, but be ready to dispatch greater numbers of planes and hammer with harder blows. The very process of attacking and killing a remorseless enemy inevitably coarsens the human fiber; and the more base that enemy, the more violent his attack, the more terrible to oneself become the consequences of resisting him.

Even those who are not engaged in actual combat will have to devote themselves with fierce military zeal to their tasks. In short: we face a grim world. And one of our chief tasks, therefore, is to offset this brutality, not by servile gestures of appeasement or cowardly hopes of flight,

232

but by intensifying our interest in those fields where man becomes most deeply human.

There are three areas, in particular, where a swift renewal in faith and act and deed must take place: these are the areas that have always been life-sustaining, life-preserving, life-forwarding. One is the family. The other is the land. And the third is the self. These three areas interlock and interpenetrate; and what is more they bottom all our other institutions, our schools and our factories and our churches; our ideals of liberty and justice and goodness and beauty. Without a revamping of our ideas and practices in these areas, without making them central, our efforts to preserve a civilized social order will be feeble and hollow, and our belated sacrifices will be in vain.

34. RE-BIRTH OF THE FAMILY

Among the family papers of a neighbor of mine is a biography of his great-grandfather; the notebook still remains in the house the old man lived in, though since that time the family itself has divided and moved away. "My dear Brother," this family book begins, "I have long wished that our children and those who shall come after them might have some knowledge of those traits in the character of our honored and dear Father, which we remember with so much pleasure, and which in some respect distinguished him from others."

This book is a happy attempt to understand and appreciate a personality, to define the values he lived by and to pass them on. In purpose and belief, it is just the opposite of those sordid debunking biographies that were fashionable in the 1920's, beginning with Lytton Strachey's series of little sneers at the eminent Victorians. And at the end, this story carries an account of the military enlistment and eventual death of the writer's own son, not yet nineteen years of age, in the Civil War. A noble record, a beautiful book, this country biography: it gives the reader a faithful picture of a family that has lived and left its mark on life.

In that simple introduction, of brother writing to brother, is the spirit of an older text: Let us now praise famous men and our fathers that begat us. This impulse is the very essence of both history and biography, or at least of any that deserve the name. The fact that such family papers are no longer produced, sometimes no longer kept and treasured, shows more than any other single fact what has happened to the very principle of family continuity in our society. Even the family Bible, with its record of births, christenings, notable events, honors, and deaths, has disappeared. If any records of family life remain, they are only those of the scattered individuals: one must search for them in the bureau that registers births, in the files of a physician or an insurance office.

In political oratory, as in pious sermons, nothing is more common than fulsome praise of the family, as the kernel of all our other social institutions. The praise is as just as it is hollow; for in the act of abandoning farmsteads for cities, and family businesses for impersonal corporate organizations that command large quantities of capital, we have permitted the economic basis of the family to be sapped.

This drift began as far back as the sixteenth century. Thomas Mann has painted a picture of later family dissolution in "Buddenbrooks"; but what he pictures as a weakening or diversion of practical judgment and economic grasp was much more than that: it was a vital and social

235

failure to provide for the continuity and higher nurture of the human stock. Life drained away from the institution that guarded life: the grave events that are centered in the family, courtship and marriage and birth and education and death, ceased to be the main core of human interest. Except among the poor, except in the quiet villages: for the poor are, in a sense, the "pagans" of our civilization, who cling in defeat and sorrow to the old homely ways.

Family events that once had social dignity and all manner of esthetic enrichment have now been reduced to purely physical processes, presided over by paid specialists. Certain vestiges of older ties are perhaps still kept up for the young, as in the celebration of birthdays; but the sense of the family unit and of family unity has been largely lost. Divorce is all too easy because the original knitting together has never been performed. In modern marriage the partners too often remain isolate atoms that resent the very suggestion that they might lose their identity in the family molecule. Each one is for himself; whereas the very essence of the family is, all for one and one for all. That had its bad side, of course, in the ancient blood feud; but even that narrow perversion of family unity still points to the essential social fact: the loyalty of kindred.

For a family to maintain its sense of itself, it must have a permanent headquarters, a permanent gathering place. It must provide opportunities for the old and the

young to meet and mix and to encounter life together. That
solidity requires land and economic foundations: at least
enough land for a house, at least enough economic support to keep the house in order. In the swift exodus from
the open country, which began in England in the eighteenth
century and by the end of the nineteenth century was
worldwide, the ancient soil of the family was deserted.
Speculators built mean little houses, and expected can-
nily to get them back when the interest on the mortgages
was not forthcoming; banks and insurance companies in-
vested in farms, and, when hard times came, seized them,
reducing the owner to a tenant or ousting him altogether.
Under current financial conditions the dwelling house was
a liability, home-ownership was a form of *in*security. The
gullible grasped at the shadow of ownership and family
independence; but society had removed the substance.

In the rush to the cities, tenements were built to house
not only the childless, but to provide quarters, cramped
and dark, for those who were founding families. Economic
conditions, crises, depressions, low wages, high land values
—all these things mocked at the security of the family.
Who could afford to bring children into the world, when
that world denied by every act that children were valuable
or families important? Prudence dictated sterilization:
fewer children to the intelligent and the provident. The
Churches, particularly the Roman Catholic Church, might
sternly resist birth control; but the statistics of population,

in Catholic countries hardly less than Protestant countries, showed how scant was their success.

Except in rural areas, where traditions die hard and life itself is uncowed, the family has remained as a vestigial institution. Among the landed aristocracy in England or the peasants in France and China, for example, the family still kept its roots in the soil, tough and unshaken; but elsewhere, and above all in the big cities, the family steadily failed, dwindling as a biological unit, losing all authority as a focus of loyalties and sentiments.

One proof of this ultimate retrogression is final. In America, in population centers of over 100,000 inhabitants, the typical family did not bear enough children to reproduce itself or keep up the population of the city without an influx of outsiders. When one opens the family closet one discovers only the skeleton. Plainly, it takes families of more than 3.2 people to reproduce the human race; even families of 4.0 people cannot fulfill their bare biological function of ensuring survival, since disease and untimely death reduce the number of those who would finally mate.

The disruption of the family has been associated with various conditions that we have permitted, in the absence of sounder values, to be unqualified in their operations.

The first was the ruthless destruction of the household arts and crafts, on the assumption that the equivalent can be purchased at a shop; and if the manufactured product is not better, it will at least provide profit to the manufacturer and his investors, instead of being merely a personal satisfaction to the members of the household. Often this change is described as labor-saving: forgetful of the fact that no person who practices an art with skill and pleasure really wants his labor saved: he wants it used.

Not merely have laborious operations, like soapmaking and woolcarding and washing clothes, disappeared in good part from even the rural home, but all the arts that gave distinction to the housewife—the preserving of fruits and vegetables, the baking of cakes, the curing of bacon and hams—have been taken over for large-scale production. Even in the country, the insistent chain store baker hammers at the door twice a week, trying to persuade my wife that her own skill is worthless; and that, if she buys his cakes, she will have more time for herself. But more time for what? For polishing the nails? Or for finding a frivolous occupation to take the place of one performed with intelligent art and smiling dignity; one capable of giving to maker and eater, the sense of communion that comes through sharing and appreciating any art.

In like fashion the enterprising business man has sought to discredit and outmode all the other crafts that once provided education and sane activity to the inhabitants of a household, or to the local craftsmen who contributed their special skill to its well-being. The result is that the modern urban household has become an intensely specialized institution for the speedy accomplishment of certain minimum physiological activities: eating, bathing, defecation, copulation, and sleep. Eating is the only one of these that requires even the partial co-operation of all the members of the household. Even here, in the big cities, a hurried breakfast is followed by a lunch outside the household. The family meets as a unit—if at all—at night; and the more prosperous the family, the less often will it meet. As for intercourse between various branches of a family, that has become perfunctory; for where, except in the open country, or perhaps the Old South, are there still homes among the middle-classes with as much as a single extra bedroom?

In consequence family life has been trivialized and impoverished; emptied of real social content and of the constant esthetic and personal values it once had. To be just a housewife is to have, in the metropolitan scheme of values, no real place in life. From the standpoint of current fashion, it is more important to write a dishonest piece of publicity or a bad poem, to spend eight hours hammering at a typewriter or sewing in a dressmaking factory, or even to stand all day at a counter in a drygoods store than to make a bed properly, diaper a baby neatly, or grow a beautiful stalk of snapdragons.

Even the daughters of the rich, who have no need for money, compete with their more necessitous sisters for jobs, so vacant do their lives seem to them, except in relation to that which alone seems to engross their interests or encompass their appetites: business success, or at least business: "real life." Instead of taking advantage of the machine to endow themselves more richly with those goods the home might specially provide, our women, young and old, have done precisely the opposite. They have not gone in for children and the skills and arts needed to educate children; they have not husbanded their energies for nurture and for passionate play. Even when they dress artfully for sexual appeal they postpone too easily the actual encounter. Obviously if modern women had the faintest notion of acting as amorously as they look, they would not smear their lips with color whose contour and outline would be spoiled by other than a peckish kiss.

No: business demands that woman adopt the smooth role; that is to say, the role of a neuter. At her best, woman brings some faint perfume of sexuality into office and factory, lightening, if only by a show of her ankle or a glimpse of her breasts, the dry routine of machine-tending. At her worst, however, she practices the really debilitating vice of carrying back into the home the efficient neutrality of the office. She is impersonal with her children, cool or slightly abstracted with her mate, too exhausted by her preoccupation with the life of industry to mind the real industry of life.

All this applies almost as much to the leisured sister of the upper suburban middle classes, who makes a business of golf or bridge, or of clubs and causes, as it does to the actual working woman. An odor of anxious antisepsis hangs even over her love-making. The only mortal error for which she feels responsible, as either an easy-going bachelor or a certificated wife, is that of being "caught"—in other words, the unforgivable sin of finding a baby growing in her womb.

There is one rough way of gauging the relative importance of any institution; and that is to observe the amount of time given to it. Though the household may remain in constant use twenty-four hours a day, the amount of time and energy given to family life, as active partnership and intercourse between parents and children, is probably in middle-class households less than that given to the motion pictures or the beauty parlor. If I exaggerate here, I only emphasize a truth.

People have thougthlessly come to accept this routine as a quite normal one; "everyone lives that way." Many even value it as a mark of a civilized life. For the great mass of urban families there is as yet no other possibility; the nearest they come to a common way of life together is in the Sunday motor ride, most of which is spent in the constriction of a car, in the benumbed state that has become so constant that motorists are not even aware of its existence. An eight-hour day in the factory or the office actually permits a man to see less of his wife and children today than a twelve-hour day did when he spent most of it in his own workshop or on his own farm.

At the end of a day of intense toil, perhaps mechanized and speeded up, the husband is tired; so, often, is the wife, especially if she have outside work today, as well as household duties. Since the school accepts the hours and schedules of the business machine as a natural pattern for its own efforts, the children are in the same fix: either taking part in school routines or chained to homework when they escape the actual confines of the school. On one day out of seven there is a chance for a common life. That is how much our civilization, during the past fifty years, has come to value the family.

What is true of the apportionment of hours holds elsewhere. Family life, in the most elementary sense of biological reproduction, is deficient; and even in the more prolific rural areas, it has come down in the United States to a rate that will produce only stability. While a thousand useful machines and futile gadgets have been poured forth by industry during the past century, the physical utilities needed to raise a family are poorer in the biggest cities today than they were in an eighteenth century village.

For what does a family need? Open plumbing? Glassed-in showerbaths? Hot and cold water? Air-conditioned heating systems? All these things might be useful, in one degree or another, provided the primary needs of family living were satisfied. But these utilities do not cover the essential family needs; quite the contrary, they claim for themselves the money that should go *directly* into those needs.

The family's basic need is for space; garden space and house space. Space for living: commodious rooms, well equipped for rest, relaxation, conversation, social intercourse; space for infants to toddle in and for runabout children to romp in; space for solitude as well as for sociability, the boudoir or "sulking" room, and the quiet study for reading and writing; space for storage, so neither physically nor spiritually will the family have to live from hand to mouth; space to store clothes and playthings; space to keep pictures safely; space to keep all manners of records, photographs, papers, diaries, drawings, so that the past will not become too shadowy; space for growing things, with a soil capable of yielding good measures of flowers, fruits, vegetables. And space is precisely what is lacking; we have been trained to do without it; our very housing authorities, fatuously thinking that they are improving conditions, boast of establishing first class mechanical equipment in the midst of fourth class living space.

Life succeeds only in an environment of life. The sterile felicity of the urban apartment house—even a model apartment house, with open areas around it and plenty of sunlight—is not, can never be, a substitute for living space. Here again we have reversed the order of human needs.

As the number of mechanical utilities has increased within the house, its space has shrunken. So in some of our desperate efforts in the United States to repair the evils of old slums we have created new ones. One would think that the designers of our metropolitan housing projects hated the family; and without being conscious of the bias, they probably do. How otherwise could they be so ignorant of its requirements; so unable imaginatively to interpret them?

35. CULTURE OF THE FAMILY

Only those fortunate enough to have had the experience of mating and raising a family under conditions that favor this occupation have any real conception of what is missing at the very core of our civilization. Most people have experienced love and parenthood, alas! under conditions that thwart them at every step: the middle classes no less than the poor. The family can flourish only by the process of continuously living in an environment which itself bears the impress of that life, favors it, responds to it, elevates it. For the family does not merely symbolize human continuity: it *is* that continuity.

It is first in the eager love of mates that the tamest personal life quickens into a fierce ecstasy: an ecstasy whose ebbing and renewal, in the long process of marriage, is one of the perpetual miracles of life. All good things take time to develop; and marriage, the best gift to lovers, requires more time for its development and completion than any other good thing. Auguste Comte well said that a lifetime was not too long for two lovers to get acquainted in.

In time, the links multiply. In the birth of their child, the man and wife perhaps first face death together; and the woman's is the braver part; for she is the soldier of marriage, and man the civilian. In the care of their children, parents relive imaginatively their own youth, in the very act of deepening all their responsibilities as adults: honey from the body of the lion! The cares, the anxieties, the sacrifices, the tensions and tribulations of parenthood hold a couple together no less than their heady joy in each other's body, their tender feelings toward all the little significant things, the clear ring of a laugh, the unconscious lift of the head, or the sobriety of a reassuring hand. Marriage may hold many joys; but it is only in suffering that has been shared that the ultimate limits of love are reached and tested.

To build a house: to plant a tree: to beget a child— these are the steps that make all the more social tasks of creation possible. Through these acts the past relives itself, starting afresh, as if love had never awakened before; and so, the future replenishes itself with hope and expectation. Even to watch a garden grow from day to day, especially if one has planted it and cared for it, deepens one's solid inner faith for living. And still more a child, or a brood of children.

The basic standards of the past century were false. The family is more important than the factory: life only avails, not the means of living. And if the family is more important, it must claim greater weight in all our calculations and time-schedules, and activities and social plans.

We must arrange wages and hours and seasons of work in order to fit the needs of the family; the family budget must take precedence over all other budgets, modify them, and make them conform to its needs. Our methods of financing and building houses, our methods of designing communities and organizing cities, must all meet the demands of the family: give it a foundation and ensure its continuity. In the course of regrouping these institutions and activities, much that was important in an age devoted to money and power will drop out, as senseless and sterile.

For unless our biological and social foundations are sound, the superstructure will be a mere makeshift, no matter how solid it may seem. The love of lovers, the nurture of parents and children together: these are fundamental things; and to bring more abundant life into the world is the only guarantee we have that our civilization will renew itself and endure. Life and more life! Life before the means of living! A higher and better life in the home, in order to offset the deprivations and sacrifices that these perilous times will inflict on all of us. Our homes and our communities must, even as physical structures, express the central importance of the family; they must be built on a human scale, and wear a friendly face. They must be designed out of love, not merely out of economy; and they must be designed to make love possible.

There have been doubtless people in every age who have

248

no vocation for family life; and of course they will remain in ours. Some of these will always devote themselves— and properly—to specialized careers; they will want to live alone, in apartments or dormitories or college halls. Even if they marry, such people will do well to avoid having children. But for more normal men and women, in the days to come, the family will be a reality of incomparably higher importance than it has been for the last century. It will not merely hold them: it will mean more to them. And why should it not? For once our modern age has re-oriented itself, it will bring to the culture of the family a wealth of scientific and imaginative interests that our ancestors did not possess.

On the physical side of family culture modern communities have already, in the very face of sterility, worked marvels. Our survival rate has kept up even though the birth rate has dropped; indeed our achievement here, particularly in the prevention of infant and child mortality, surpasses every other race and country for which there is a trace of a record. We have no need for that shameless animal fecundity of which the race boasted in the past. Nor need women submit to that exhaustion and early death that so often overtook them in the past, when they produced, possibly, twelve babies in as many years. At the end of that time they often yielded their own life in childbirth without having given to the world any larger number of survivors than their more artfully sterile sisters today.

There is no doubt, in America, of the superior physical health of children who have been bred carefully, in families that possess both economic means and affectionate intelligence. Their moral and esthetic and social life, however, is not so indisputably in advance of past periods; even the utmost efforts of deliberate education, in well-equipped schools, have only succeeded in part in offsetting the debilitating effects of our too mechanized environment and our too impassive routine.

But the machine itself has been redressing the balance a little in favor of the family. One does not wish to imitate Mr. Ralph Borsodi's attempts to supplant a mixed economy with a pure household economy—the latter should be a last desperate alternative to starvation—but he is right in thinking that small machines and utilities adapted to household needs may be just as efficient as big ones, horsepower for horsepower, man-days for man-days. With that help, certain valuable crafts and skills will come back again to the household.

In addition, the household has become a new focus for contact with the outside world: the radio, the telephone (presently television), reduce the isolation of the home. The wide world is now but a neighboring village. But this development has been too much on the passive side: the family receives but it does not as yet give. The phonograph is highly to be prized; but it is not a substitute for the part singing of motets and madrigals that intensified the life of the Elizabethan household in England.

The culture of the family requires time, patience, and fuller participation by all its members; and for its personal sustenance, interest must be awakened on its spiritual side: its history and biography. The antiquarian search for a family tree is too often the lowest snobbism; but the actual planting and cultivating of the family tree is a different matter. That is worthy of everyone's highest skill and immediate attention.

In America we have a great advantage over the people who lived even a hundred and fifty years ago. In contrast to them, we are a nation of literates: reading and writing are our minimum accomplishments. So for us the widespread keeping of family records is at least mechanically an easy job: spiritually it will require immense effort, before we pour into the work all the love and skill that it demands. The writing of journals, psychological records, and family histories beginning with the here and now should be one of the most grateful tasks for parents: the gathering of souvenirs, memorabilia, drawings, the recording of anecdotes and stories—all these things will build up that past which will form a bridge, over the most turbid autumnal torrent, to a firmer, finer future.

Some of our young people will die before their time, fighting barbarian forces or combating famine and plague.

251

Those who survive them in the family will bear the loss more easily if they do not vanish completely, leaving behind only a few fading photographs. The richer the record, the less of them will die. That is the consolation of the writer and the artist when he faces death: let it also be the consolation of parents and children. Life becomes precious again in the family: let us therefore live and relive its best moments: first in action, then in memory.

There are other grounds for creating a book of the family: scientific no less than sentimental. The completer the records of a personal life, the easier it is to retrace mistaken paths, or to put together dispersed fragments. At critical moments in life, before a marriage or a new departure in one's vocation, it is good to go back into the past, in order to have a running start for the leap one must take.

There is nothing that gives depth to life more than such a conscious piling up of experience; nothing that serves as a better guide, in periods of tension and crisis, than a renewal of these sources of one's personal growth. Half of those buried experiences the psychoanalyst seeks to spade up from the compost of rotted memories, might be available, in surer form, from the records of the family book. Those are the true confessions that would replace the tawdry magazines devoted to this theme. Such books would of course vary from the most bare and simple annals, done conscientiously but stupidly—and neverthe-

252

less valuable in their own degree—to the truly imaginative record in which the novelist and the psychologist would blend their skills to a new task in biography.

The plea that there is no time for such observation and such record cannot be defended. There is always time for what we think worth doing. People today find time for frequent visits to the motion pictures, endless repetitions of radio broadcasts, and interminable hours of wheeling along glib highways. They are well-equipped and ready for any kind of passive, semi-automatic activity; provided it makes no serious demands on them. Our time is our own: to use well or ill. If people were concerned with their personal relations, their love relations, and their family relations as seriously as they are concerned with a more mechanized routine they would have plenty of time for it. What has been lacking is interest. For the majority of the passing generation, domestic life was just not living.

Yet was it not absurd that our children should grow up without ever knowing their parents even in retrospect? That parents should often involve themselves in heavy labor on behalf of their children, without having the opportunity to participate as sympathetic observers in their growth? The parents themselves miss those precious moments when growth reveals itself in a gesture, an act, or a sudden word; and the child in turn misses the feeling of stability he needs through the mere upright presence of those whom he loves and respects. This task of watchful intercourse cannot be entirely transferred to teachers; though of course there must be something of the parent in every good teacher, as there is something of the teacher in every competent parent.

I recall the confession of a young German girl who had lived through the desperate inflation period in Germany. Her parents had been rich; and she scarcely knew them in their period of prosperity, since her time was spent with governesses, tutors, chauffeurs. As a result of the inflation they lost their fortune; and instead of living in a luxurious house, with a greenhouse that provided flowers, they moved to a cottage near the country, and they used to go out as a family for walks afield over the weekend, picking wild flowers by the roadside. She looked back to that period as the most enjoyable one in her life: one that gave her for the first time what she as a child had desired—two interested and amusing parents.

Need I add what happened when "prosperity" came back? As soon as money returned, the real goods of life diminished. Her parents, despite their own obvious pleasure in this simple existence, dropped back into the routine of fashionable society. For my own part, I watched the same process happen among my comfortable neighbors in Sunnyside, Long Island, when the economic depression hit them. Their economic state worsened; but their domestic state often brightened. Unemployment in many households meant that children had the privilege of playing with their father at other times than the frayed end of a day.

Here, then, is the very core of a fresh culture: the cultivation of the family. Biological cultivation: care and responsibility in mating: development of the erotic ritual: rational spacing of births: and finally a new joy in fecundity itself, even if the coming of an extra child means the curtailment of some familiar mechanical luxury. The times in which we live will require the strictest asceticism in the purchase of a hundred oddments we once thought essential: even those who can afford motor cars will have to watch their gas. But in compensation, every family that is conscious of itself as a family, conscious of its unity and its destiny, will have an opportunity to enjoy the wealth of the poor: children.

Social cultivation of the family springs out of this biological root. The old arts of the household, from cooking to good manners; and the new arts of the household, including the exquisite nurture and observation of the young—these arts will stimulate vital interests and beget more durable joys. They will utilize everyone's emotional and intellectual capacities, up to the limits of his growth. The family book and the personal record will accompany this nurture; and so people will hand on, first from day to day, and then from generation to generation, the oldest and toughest of human traditions—and the youngest and dearest.

255

The great capacity of the Jews and the Chinese, above all other peoples, to survive the cancerous attacks of dehumanized power has derived from their sense of the family: their loyalty to the generations behind them and those yet to come. If we recover that sense, we Americans, nothing will shake us; no disaster that may in the meanwhile lie in wait for us will cause us to lose our faith in what is still to come.

Bernard Shaw once contemptuously called the United States a nation of villagers. One may now inscribe those words proudly on our banners. To the extent that we are still a nation of villagers, we have the homely traditions that will serve us as a nucleus in our efforts to turn this wry metropolitan economy inside out, in order that its machines may serve life instead of defeating it.

A nation of villagers: that is to say, a nation of neighbors and families—Good! There is a foundation to build upon, and a goal to work toward. Except where commercial farming and high finance have displaced rural life with one-crop farms, and left behind a sour and sapless life, the open country still holds the germ of a more vital economy. More than half our people are still within reach of mother earth; and already the growth of our cities during the last decade shows a slowing up.

We have enough people on the land, and enough of the tradition of the family vaguely left, to form the core of a new economy to displace the now-discredited economy of paper profits, paper joys, and paper wealth. Out on the pastures and the prairies, in the cornland and the grassland and the wheatland and the vineland, life still holds it own: the cows with their calves, the mares with their foals, and mothers with their children.

Be fruitful, not prudent: increase and multiply your children, not the ciphers in your bank account. Those are the sane words for our time. The girls and boys who marry young will taste young love's first tartness; and have that for contrast with the richer, juicier years of old experience. The young people who dare to have a child, though they must use a basket for a crib, will have a better reward than if they save their dollars for a swell layette and crib and carriage—and miss the baby. Those who have no old home to look back to, may have it still in the home that their children and their grandchildren will look back to. Life will go on through the dark days and the scrimping days because the real demands of life are simple and direct—much more direct and simple than those who see only the complicated scaffolding of our power-civilization have dared to dream. When one removes that heavy scantling, the outlines of life's structure itself are plain.

The culture of the family will be our first great simplification of life; our first act of restoring faith for the living. He who has dropped a seed into a garden or into a woman's womb is ready to fight for the right of that seed to grow and fulfill itself. He who has stood by it and nurtured it is himself in the line of growth. Many other conditions are necessary for the good life; but this bottoms them all.

36. ROOTS IN THE REGION

Men are attached to places as they are attached to families and friends. When these loyalities come together, one has the most tenacious cement possible for human society.

One of the great effects of the age of discovery and the age of invention that followed it was the worldwide displacement of millions of people. In Europe, they left lands that their families had occupied for hundreds of years, sometimes a good thousand at least. They dropped their old associations, with this river, with that mountain, with a castle hanging over a crag or a group of Church towers pricking the sky over mist-hung marsh; they left the earth that had molded them to find a place for themselves in the new lands. First they trickled into the New World, trading and fighting and shrewdly seeking profits; then the trickle, in the nineteenth century, became a spring flood of people carrying in its turbid course not merely human bodies but the very silt and detritus of their cultures.

Millions came to America: particularly, perhaps, those with shallow roots, or those whose rootlets had been killed by political despotism and economic oppression. Some of them struck root; from Massachusetts to Georgia there are families that stayed put from scratch: groups that identified themselves with a particular spot of soil and sky and water, and bear its marks on speech and skin. Others moved on, settled, became restless, kept moving: sometimes they turned their backs to the soil and found themselves a place in the new cities.

The will to move was there; so were the vehicles; people came by ocean steamship, and moved on by wagon and railroad. Mere ease in locomotion aided this transplanting of individuals and groups; the open land, so plentiful and so cheap, tempted them, too. Like a child confronted with too many toys at one time, they grabbed everything, stuck to nothing, and kept on changing over.

A certain uniformity in superficial things abetted this movement in the United States: a common system of government that by mid-century covered a good part of the continent: laws and canned goods and sheet-iron roofs and transport vehicles and plumbing, being all uniform, kept the restless pioneers from feeling any shock when they slipped from one environment to another. Underneath, regional differences continued to exist; but, after 1850, national fashions and a national market began to minimize them.

Quickly enough these new immigrants became patriotic; but, unlike the older families and regions, the patriotism of the newcomers was attached to institutions rather than to places. It had to do with the machinery for voting,

260

making laws, imposing taxes. Hence patriotism became entangled in a quite abstract conception: political uniformity and national unity. After the War between the States, it was finally established that laws that are passed by the Congress of the United States must apply uniformly to all citizens, without regard to local conditions and regional characteristics. This either put the burden for local legislation on the separate states, which often had no geographic or social identity, or made it necessary to recognize differences within the national pattern by subterfuge and hypocrisy. Local politics became shabby and down at the heels; only national government mattered.

Another result of this thinning out of a community's natural loyalties to the land, was the fact that patriotism tended to identify itself with the reactionary and the old-fashioned: a little like religion, it reserved its ceremonies for occasional use; piously permitting the wealth of the country to be hastily extracted by those who had an eye on the main chance. Even today, at the hint of a national emergency, the first instinct of many selfish people is to suggest an immediate abandonment in the name of patriotism of any laws or acts that restrain the privileges or emoluments of their group.

Surely there is not the least reason why patriotism should be monopolized by reactionaries. Neither is there any reason why the only kind of patriotism that should be recognized is that which is identified with the sovereign

261

national state. On this point, one feels that the Southern regions lost a war in fighting for a poor cause that one might well have wished them to win had they been fighting solely for the right to retain their individualities as communities. Sectionalism became a word of reproach after the Civil War. People tried to forget Hawthorne's wise dictum, to the effect that New England was as large a spot of earth as he could love. As a result our politics lacked love: love of country was honored by words of praise on the Fourth of July, not by actions every day in the year.

Now patriotism is a universal attribute of normal people. It is grounded in space and time; that is, in the actual soil and landscape of a region, and in the experience of life that, in retrospect, constitutes its people's history. The deepest source of this love of country is neither law nor property, although they play a part in qualifying it: the ultimate source is the land as land, the sky as sky, the people as people.

—The red soil of the Shenandoahs in Virginia, with the apple trees whose boughs skirt the ground; the granite hills of Vermont with their white churches, stiff against the north winds, honest and unyielding as only fanatics are honest and unyielding; the undulating meadow land of Iowa, with curves as delicate as a pea's tendrils; or the hard primeval clarity and the enveloping loneliness of the desert, from the white alkali of Utah to the red canyons of Arizona.

These are samples of our regions: samples of backgrounds, to be filled out with the stories that are told and the pictures painted, by the houses that are fabricated, by all that the hand of man has added. All that—and the people themselves, speaking an English speech that now glides over the tongue and now clogs it, that halts at the nose or escapes half formed through soft and lazy lips. The plow and the lariat; the yoke that holds the maple bucket; the dusty threshing machine; the filling station and the relentless assembly line; the steel mill and skyscraper that is itself a gigantic filing case, holding other filing cases. The things that men love because they are easy, and those they love because they are hard and the men can take it—the hayfield at 110 degrees or the rolling mill at 120.

These are the sights and experiences and places and ways and tools that make the indelible reality of our American patriotism. But in its best sense, patriotism is always narrow and intense: close to one's family, one's village or city and the land around. Regional sentiments spring out of a settled way of life: deep roots in the soil itself.

In the restless movings about of the last two centuries, this essential relation between the human spirit and its background was derided, underestimated, sometimes overlooked. Had it been acknowledged for what it was worth, it might have stayed the pioneer in his very act of pulling up stakes and moving away. The land itself was looted and mined because men did not yet love it sufficiently; nor did they heed what sort of life they would leave for those who came after them. What had posterity done for them? Where men shifted so easily no cultural humus formed; no human tradition thickened. Did the farmers who became rich in Iowa after the World War stay in their state, and devote their leisure and their savings to its common life? By report, just the opposite happened: they uprooted themselves from their lovely landscape, to become a herd of flighty, money-obsessed people in California.

But now the period of terrestrial exploration is over. All over the world men are beginning to settle down and take root. Or rather, that was what was happening before the new fascist barbarians began to tear men away from their dear lands. In America the process of settlement reached its first apogee along the Eastern seaboard between 1800 and 1850: the period of the Golden Day. Now it is beginning over again; and what happened in New England in the period of Hawthorne's and Emerson's youth, when every village had its history and its lovers of tradition, is at last starting to happen in every part of the country.

The reason is plain. Great continental states or empires are too big to be in intimate relations with men's daily needs and desires; great financial corporations and administrative organizations are likewise too impersonal by nature and cover too small a fragment of life, even when their intentions are humane. But there must be a focus for communal attachment, bigger than the family or the city, smaller than the country or all mankind; and the surest source of that sustaining kind of patriotism is the region.

The conscious recovery of regional roots has been going on in the world for almost a hundred years: indeed, if one counts in New England, where the roots had not been severed, it goes back longer than this. This movement is sometimes confused with nationalism; but it has a more local and concentrated objective, except in places where the regional and the national boundaries coincide, as in Ireland. Actually, the conscious re-establishment of the local and historical tradition first was the work of a group of Provençal poets in France; the Félibrigistes. But what happened in France, once the most centralized of modern states, has been happening everywhere else.

To create a balanced life in each region has become a contribution to local self-respect and to world-culture. We must concentrate our loyalties before we can expand them; we must have the practice of dressing and keeping the land, and embodying our love for it in the very way we fashion the buildings that we build. Regionalism, then, grows out of an immediate fondness for a soil and a way of life: for the language and the cultural products of a group of people, intimately connected with a particular landscape. As it develops, regionalism embraces more and more the political and economic aspects of a community. When a people, like the Jews, lacks a regional home it restores its loss through dreams and utopias, like that of Zion. At the first opportunity it returns, even under hardships and handicaps, to its land. The alternative to regionalism is not nationalism, but dispersion.

In America, regionalism has two sides to it; one, the conservation movement, connects with the use of resources, with the balance of nature, with the intelligent exploitation of water power, minerals, forests, and the like. The other side is the cultural and sentimental side. Each of these movements lacks something that the other supplies; for a sentimental regionalism, that dreams dreams without putting a foundation under them, must finally lose its own self-respect and be pushed over by more aggressive economic and political interests originating outside the region, sometimes hostile to it, sometimes simply callous. The conservation of resources, on the other hand, is hardly a program to stir men's blood: one might as well intone the *World Almanac* for inspiration. Politics is always a battleground of interests; and a low, anti-social interest can be combated only by another interest that shows a higher human potential.

Conservation, it is true, has had many modest triumphs in America, ever since the first National Parks were set aside as public domains. Yet it is hard to imagine any considerable body of our youth being willing to die for the ideal of conservation. At times, where the imagination is kindled by a visible threat, the need for conservation may persuade a university town, like Eugene, Oregon, to buy up a neighboring mountain to keep the forest on it from being cut down completely. But one does no injustice to the conservation program to say that, admirable as it is, it has not awakened anything like a universal sense of obligation.

The same observation applies in part to the valuable studies of the National Resources Committee and the various co-operating State Boards. They have every indispensable characteristic, many of these studies, except the breadth of imagination, the human sentiment, and the co-operative understanding that would bring them to life.

The regionalist movement, at the same time, has shown a characteristic weakness, which was not lacking in the earliest stages and has not yet been completely sloughed off. This is visible in the South and in New England— the tendency to hark back too fondly to its image in the past. In New England this makes the local patriots think highly of their Puritan or Georgian architecture, but to forget the noble-looking factories of Fall River and Lowell, and to ignore the freshest contributions of all before the twentieth century, the cottage architecture of Richardson. It makes the regionalist think that old iron forges were indeed worthy of another generation, but new steel mills

267

are just the horrid present. It even makes people take pride in local warts, because they are local, and to forget the unblemished face, because it is universal.

Sometimes, then, the regional patriot tries to isolate the local unit itself from the great stream of history, which carried it along, and gave it its larger meaning. The historical basis of development, which should serve as a point of departure, becomes a resting place, a trap that lures the regionalist into attempting to return to a past that has ceased to exist. Under this delusion history becomes a utopia; the good days are always behind; and instead of his undertaking the perpetual reconquest of the environment, in terms of all man's accumulating inventions, purposes, and desires, the regionalist contents himself with a dream of archaic reconstruction—as if life could be lived in a museum.

Even on the purely practical side, regionalism tends often unconsciously to misdirect its aims to an obsolete past. Witness the attempt on the part of individual states to erect trade barriers against other states. What is this but a blind chaotic effort to go back to a past when natural obstacles created a narrow, self-sufficient economy? The means which would serve to create a balanced region demand quite a different kind of planning: planning which would embrace a continental or a global area, and would not merely provide for an intensive, many-sided development of resources and industries within the local area, but would at the same time provide a planetary organization of markets, for the orderly interchange of surpluses, specialties, and highly localized resources. This not merely means cultivating all that one has; it also means reaching out for all the things that the region lacks. That principle applies on both the economic and the cultural levels.

We in America have often taken the view, to use Carlyle's brutal words about Whitman, that we must be a great people because we live in a large country. We have acted as if the mere abundance of natural resources and raw materials was any guarantee that we would utilize them in a rational, purposeful fashion. Similarly we have created units of local government and administration, our states and counties, without worrying in the least whether the land enclosed by their legal boundaries constitutes any sort of organic unit, in history and geography, to which men's natural loyalties and affections would cling. Hence we have river valleys like the Connecticut, the Ohio, the Mississippi, and the Columbia, in which the very unity that is promoted by a river system is destroyed by the mapmaker's ingenious nonsense of calling a river a boundary line because the black line that represents it on the map looks like one.

Our belief that resources by themselves make us great has another serious defect. It gives but feeble counsel to those parts of the country that nature has endowed sparingly with wealth, as in our grand desert regions, or in

269

those parts which war and human erosion have left blighted, as in certain regions of the South.

In renewing our relations with the land we must not be deceived by the specious belief that abundance is the sole guarantee of culture. Dearth and poverty are sometimes more effective challenges to human powers than is wealth; witness the case of Holland, which lacked, so to say, ground to stand on. Out of their poverty the Netherlanders won from the sea and reclaimed for agriculture one of the richest and most thriftily used soils in Europe; and as a by-product they achieved a skill in hydraulic engineering and building that gave them pre-eminence in the seventeenth century, both in technics and science. Thanks to their original poverty, they created a garden where four hundred years before a handful of fishermen kept a bare hold on a spit of sand. The same is true of our salt desert, Utah; which provided the stimulus for the most provident and politically adroit piece of colonization that the country can boast.

At best, resources are capital reserves. It is well to have rich land, a plentiful water supply, a heavy forest cover, an abundance of metals and minerals. But none of these things is indispensable; and the mere quantity of resources does not determine the purposes and ends of a regional culture. Purpose rather determines the quantity that shall be used. Where money purposes have been consistently uppermost, resources that should have lasted half a mil-

270

lennium have been gutted out in twenty years. Without vision, therefore, both resources and people perish.

The Grand Coulee Dam, for example, is a piece of imaginative planning of genuine value, on the level of technics: it promises potentially to transform a region of difficulty into a region of increment; and it does this with a breath-taking adroitness in commanding natural possibilities. Thanks to the dam and its hydro-electric works and its coming irrigation system, there is the opportunity of creating a desert culture that will offer far higher possibilities for the life abundant than the half-arid, thinly settled region that now exists.

But is anything like the same quality of imagination available as yet on the human and communal level? To ask that question is to make the answer ludicrous. The new resources that will be created in eastern Washington by the new dam demand an heroic order of public service, a generation disciplined to creative thinking and co-operative public action, a corps of architects, educators, poets and philosophers, no less than farmers, agricultural experts, and engineers. Do they exist in the Pacific Northwest except in minute samples? No. Do they exist even in the United States? Only a handful.

We are not handicapped by lack of opportunity to exploit our regional resources; we are burked by lack of creative purposes. Our love for the land is a lazy one. Our civilization as a whole is partly parasitic on both the machine and nature; it has yet to create a pattern for regional living and the means that would make that pattern effective.

Meanwhile our young people are starving for lack of real tasks and vital opportunities. Many of them live like sleepwalkers, apparently in contact with their environment, but actually dead to everything but the print of the newspapers, the blare of the radio, or the flickering shadows on the screen. Is it any wonder that they seek to dull their frustrations in speed and other forms of excited anesthesia; that they vote crooners into positions of political responsibility, follow screeching hysterics who promise to give them something to do, or are both bewildered and fascinated by an ignoble and addled personality, like Hitler?

Work alone is no answer to this frustration; not even part of an answer. Work at good wages, with social security and an ultimate pension, seems a promise of paradise only to a starved, anxiety-ridden body. For the very nature of the work itself, its impersonality, its automatism, its imperviousness to human requirements, makes it almost as much the cause of frustration as unrelieved idleness.

But the young will care for their regional home if they have a part in creating it. They will live an effective and responsible life if once they have an opportunity to see and feel and touch and listen to all those activities that belong to their native scene. Why should the young people not have their first experience of public service on work that serves for local improvement? They should help clear the slums, as well as study housing; they should help plant the forests as well as study conservation; it is our school children, and not the dreary and defeated Joads, who should have a turn at camping and picking the peaches and apples—on terms that will wipe out every last vestige of economic despotism in places like the Imperial Valley. It is our youngsters nearing military age who should be toughened off in lumber camps, on fishing boats, behind the hay-wagon and the threshing machine, on the road gang and in the quarry.

Such regional experiences—and inter-regional experiences—are the very basis of communal health. They begin and end with a loving awareness of one's environment, comradely intercourse with and participation in the lives of one's fellows: a role in the regional drama, and a part, if only a super's part, in regional history.

The Civilian Conservation Corps, and the various activities of the National Youth Administration, have made a brave start here. But the chief defect of both these organizations is that they deal only with those who are unemployed: a segregated class. We need a Civilian Conservation Corps that will enlist, at least for a year's service, every girl and boy in the country. This corps should be organized on a regional basis; but there should be special opportunities, for those most adventurous and capable, of taking on work in other parts of the country. This would be a true circulation of the élite.

Such a corps will become the very backbone of our new democracy. By mixing classes and groups, it will undermine the dreary caste system that now pushes its snobberies and impertinences right into many of our public high schools, and has already left dead areas of social isolation throughout our once largely democratic country. The work of this larger C.C.C. will eventually include far more than reforestation: the Quaker work camps, for example, have pointed the way to wider social efforts.

These youngsters will not merely reforest our barren slopes and fight insect pests; they will plant trees along bare roads, for shade and beauty, pushing the trail of Johnny Appleseed beyond the Alleghenies; they will keep up our otherwise too costly parkways and help extend them further; they will clear out the rural slums, trim up the rundown edges of our landscape, and bring music, art, and personal beauty into parts of the country that are now ugly, infamous, and unfit for human habitation.

Such universal service was advocated earnestly a generation ago by one of the stoutest exponents of American individualism and self-reliance, Liberty Hyde Bailey: a name that every American with a rural background must respect to the point of reverence. Without such a collective instrument of democratic service as this Civilian Corps, our young people must remain at loose ends, tied to petty tasks, cramped by lack of a horizon, never quickened to the opportunities for comradeship and bold pioneering that our country offers—offers and *demands* if we are to create a worthier civilization.

All the new tasks of regional improvement claim more than routine service; and the performance of them in youth will be a discipline in public duties that our democracy has long lacked. Those who have camped together, traveled together, worked together, and exchanged ideas and matched beliefs while scrubbing their clothes or jawing over a campfire, will have a new stake in their country and a new confidence in themselves. The hardships they will encounter in the service, the lack of domestic comforts, the lean days of backbreaking, sometimes ugly work, the individual's occasional loneliness far from his own roof—all this will breed a toughness that no other mode of education, short of war, can produce, except under conditions that permanently stultify the spirit.

And mark this: to be able to stand routine and hardship is an absolute necessity of personal development. All play and no work is as debilitating a prescription for education as all work and no play is for life itself. Every citizen should have, as a condition of his holding the full privileges of citizenship, a spell of disciplined collective work: bread-work, earth-work, man-work: work devoted to improving the face of the land, to combating the destructive natural forces that are in action, to salvaging and redeeming for civilization those families and communities that are near to relapsing into barbarism, out of their poverty and isolation.

That way lies a democracy of comrades, as staunch in peace as in war; and that way, too, lies the intimate knowledge of our human background that will guide effectively our efforts to make the community itself a high work of art.

On his weekend walks over the Boston hinterland the planner, Charles Eliot, Jr., when only a schoolboy, laid out in his mind the great Metropolitan Parks System of Boston: an outstanding feat of the imagination. When such deliberate first-hand contact with nature and man becomes a common element in American citizenship and education, there will be no lack of opportunities for our youth. If their elders falter, youth will have the discipline and insight and experience that will fit them to deal with political realities. They will be ready for more vital changes in our institutions than the copy-book communism that is now offered to them can suggest.

In short, education begins at home; and one of the outstanding advantages of identifying oneself with one's regional home, native or adopted, lies in the land's capacity to provide the materials for an effective education. Regional survey and regional service—these are the chief ingredients for a responsible citizenship; and laboring *on*

276

the land, laboring *with* the land, laboring *for* the land, should be the first initiation of every boy and girl in their duties toward the whole community.

Before we Americans can effectively enter in a wider partnership on the basis of a worldwide civilization—and that after all is one of the prime meanings of a long religious and scientific development—we must first of all strike root. It is by regional cultivation, not by the legal tokens of citizenship, that patriotism in the deepest sense, now vitiated by all manner of cynicism, will come back to us. Without it, the ideas of democracy can have no body.

Already we have made a serious start here. That love for the sea and the soil that made Ryder, Homer, and Fuller the very breath of New England has spread outward over the country. Up and down the land young men and women are looking at their country and painting it. They have gone forth with kodaks and motion picture cameras, showing its woes, proclaiming its beauties: they have floated down the Mississippi and followed the Plow That Broke the Plains. There has been a stir during these last ten years: more vital culture has come out of the sobering poverty of the depression than ever came out of the riotous period of so-called prosperity in the twenties.

Above all, our W.P.A. projects in music, drama, literature, and the graphic and plastic arts—and not least the great series of state and regional guidebooks—have shown what new energies these regional interests can unleash, even in their first bare beginnings. Out of this will grow a pride of life, an eagerness, a deep and intimate knowledge, and a sentiment of possession: qualities that will bring within the realm of practical operation a multitude of projects that now lack understanding and backing. And partly out of this new knowledge and pride, many half-baked or irregional projects, like skyline drives and National Parks developed as primeval Coney Islands, will be passionately rejected.

In this mood, one can repeat again, with an even more solemn sense of obligation, Thoreau's question:

Who would not rise to meet the expectation of the land?

A new generation is already at hand, eager to answer this question. They have tasted their native soil and found it good; and they have dreams for it that gallop far ahead of any politician's promise. They will write for their region a platform no politician would dare to stand on yet: the restoration of the land to the people and the people once more to the land.

If old property lines and mortgages and franchises and vested interests get in the way, these firm young hands will give the tractor a little more gas and push over such ancient snags. This solid partnership, with loving knowledge to guide it, will cultivate the entire countryside and rebuild and rearrange the cities. That will be only a beginning.

Our regions—from the heights of Mt. Hood, where the moccasin flower blows, to the swampy Everglades of Florida—expect more than this of us Americans; and we will not be loath to rise still higher, once we get a start.

37. GROWTH OF THE PERSON

During the past few centuries men have submitted to a curious denial of personality. They have expanded the impersonalized, mechanized, and institutional portions of their existence; and they have narrowed the province of the personal. Sometimes they complain: We have no time left to ourselves. That is exactly the inevitable upshot of their efforts.

This systematic surrender of the personality has not gone on without protest. The poets and artists of modern times have fought resolutely against it, because any such surrender is for them nothing short of suicide. It is this belief in the personality, more than any other characteristic, that has made the artist seem queer and that has aroused a combat, more than a century old, with the philistines.

By a process of compensation, certain arts like painting and music, absorbing much of the religious impetus that had left the churches, have thriven mightily, at the moment when the role of art itself was shrunken. Images, once the universal accompaniment of a humane life, were more and more restricted to special galleries and museums; and music, driven out of the Victorian drawing room, driven even out of its last stronghold, the family parlor, with its piano, took refuge in a special sanctuary, the concert hall. As the popular forms of all these arts became increasingly banal and trashy, a fresh intensification, an ardent concentration, an immensely vaster emotional range, was opened up.

But who could receive these new gifts? Only a few highly developed personalities. And who produced them? A handful of divine fanatics and saints. When one considers the obstacles and diversions, the output in the arts during the past two centuries has been immense: for those centuries include Bach and Handel at one end and Debussy and Stravinsky at the other; they include Chardin and Daumier, Goya, Cézanne, Renoir, and Picasso; they include the childlike poems of Blake and the last subtleties of Rilke.

But although art, with a torrential energy of its own, swept on in its course, during a period when men boasted most loudly about the yards of calico and the tons of woodpulp they produced, nevertheless it exists in modern society under severe restrictions. Many of our higher activities are curbed by the fact that so much of our energies, as human beings, are absorbed by non-personal and non-esthetic routines. The mere fact that the majority of people go to a theater or a concert hall at the end of a long working day explains in good part the quality of the drama they demand. They are unable to face the intense, delicate, exacting experiences of high art. Jaded, they need stimuli; or they are irritated and they need sedatives.

In this respect, the traditional religions with their day of rest devoted strictly to contemplation, and their historic or seasonal festivals, were far more favorable to the finer cultivation of the personality. The production of the tragic dramas in Athens took place on a series of public holidays. People gave themselves as whole-heartedly to this emotional and religious experience as they did, when the holidays were over, to the dickering of the market place. The effect of leisure on our machine-ridden society is chiefly to promote other forms of purely consumptive activity, other modes of passive acceptance and ritualistic vacuity.

What applies to the contemplative arts applies equally well in another domain of personal development: the arts of action. The dance, gymnastic, above all courtship and sexual expression, show the same deficiencies, and the same strained tendencies to narrow over-compensation. Without leisure, freshness, energy, all these arts lose their inner impetus; and their performers must be excited to activity by the negative stimulus of ill-health, by competitive record-breaking, or by preliminary bouts of strong liquor. Yet these arts are surely as central to life as the most beneficent practical activity. To fail in these departments is to reduce oneself to a nonentity; and the attempt to create a good community by adding nonentities together is like attempting to add up a column of zeroes: the result is still zero.

Now the fact is that a self-governing, self-acting, and self-respecting person is the very foundation of a democratic society. Nonentities must inevitably submit to despots; lacking personal self-confidence, they will identify themselves with a single individual to whom, collectively, they assign all freedom, all power, all wisdom, all the qualities that they fail to find in themselves or fail, even when they are present, to nourish and discipline.

Here one sees the deep wisdom in Walt Whitman's concern for persons; the creation of persons is the first and last task of a democracy. This nucleus, this identity, must be present; the sense of the self must be developed to the full, by all the arts that men command, in order that the community shall not be a mere dust-heap of unidentifiable atoms. It is lack of self-respect that turns fascists, at the word of command, from passively stupid people to actively malignant ones, capable of any kind of sadism. It is lack of self-respect that permits communists on the official reversal of the "party line" to proclaim with robot-like precision that the truth they passionately defended yesterday has become a reprehensible lie. Such people may brazenly attempt to outface those around them because they have never faced themselves. Facing themselves, they would indeed die of self-contempt—if their self were not, in fact, a stunted undeveloped thing. The minds of fascists and communists are blank paper, waiting from moment to moment for the party rubber stamp.

Faith for living is ultimately bound up with the capacity for self-development and self-reliance. The self is central, and all the arts and ideologies that sustain the personality become, by that very fact, central. To expand the person is the only possible way to escape the eternal tyranny of things and institutions, and limit the irrational arrogance of smaller selves, selves that, because of their very lack of organic development, attain a sort of one-sided vitality. The latter never achieve humility; and their nearest approach to that higher state of the self, which is called selflessness, is complete abdication.

38. DISCIPLINE OF WORK

The fragmentary man, concentrating upon some narrow proficiency, eager for power in the form of riches or direct command over other men, eager for it sometimes in the surrogate form of scientific learning, was a product of capitalism and militarist ideals. These ideals progressively dominated the life of Western man. They span the period from the end of the Middle Ages to the present day: from Machiavelli to Mussolini, from Fugger to the Fuehrer, from the robber barons of late feudalism to the robber barons of late imperialism.

This fragmentary personality was conjured into existence at a particular moment of European history, when the terrestrial and mechanical conquest of the globe beckoned to those who were bored with smaller victories. The new man was trained to command, not to co-operate: or to obey, not to participate. Whole men, full men, would not work well as cogs in the factory, the bureaucracy, or the army; their very capacity for becoming human, their very potentialities for fulfilling a human destiny, stood in the way of this one-sided efficiency.

Now there were three places where the ideal of the whole man was lost in our program of education. The first loss occurred early in the Renaissance. This was the displacement of manual skill and the daily discipline of manual effort in the training of so-called educated people. The inability to work with the hands became a point of pride among the educated classes. In the meanwhile, a surrogate form of manual effort, the use of arms, or later, sport, came to take the place of more useful manual activity. But by that very fact labor was made trivial and sport itself lost some of its special quality, that of being irresponsibly playful, through a tendency toward professionalism. Our pioneer habits and needs, our once predominantly rural background, slowed up this fashionable tendency in America; but by the end of the last century even Americans succumbed.

The restoration of manual labor as a daily discipline should, I believe, stand high in any attempt at personal integration. Already, psychiatrists have come to realize the uses of carpentry, weaving, painting, modeling, or gardening in the cure of nervous disorders. But why should one fall ill before one is provided with an adequate diet? It is time to realize, as the great teachers from Benedict of Nursia onward have recognized, that manual labor is perhaps equally important in the prevention of disorder: a constant means for maintaining organic balance and spiritual equipoise. Gardens are cheaper than asylums; likewise more rewarding.

In active manual labor the body becomes well exercised,

the hand and eye co-ordinated, the spirit accepts the discipline of routine, whilst in the concrete activity itself—a bed of flowers, a path hewn through the woods, a rug or a cabinet—the worker achieves a result far more rewarding than the abstract numerical score which is his sole reward for the utmost effort at sport. Above all, in co-operative tasks undertaken by a whole group, the worker achieves comradeship; and by buckling down to the meanest occupations he thereby widens his understanding of all the humbler modes of life.

Brotherhood in labor is the most fundamental kind of brotherhood, after that of the family. The Masonic orders recognized this fact when they took over in ceremony the forms, inherited or simulated, that were used by the old Mason Guilds. But unfortunately modern Masonry was a product of the eighteenth century, and in the amateurish spirit in which the ladies of the French court lived in cottages and posed as dairymaids and shepherdesses, the Masons only posed as workers. Behind that sacred gesture was the god of all respectable people—a god without hands.

In Europe, during the last century, some of the physical and social discipline of work was shared by the whole male community in the army. That was a double limitation; not merely did it limit work to the preparatory arts of war; it excluded half the human race. But here and there people existed who saw, as Tolstoy and Morris had long before discovered in their personal lives, the real values that were involved. One of them, a pioneer educator, Dr. Eugen Rosenstock-Huessy, founded the labor camp movement in Germany in order to bring together, in a close working comradeship, young men from the country and those from the city, the intellectual and the manual worker, the mechanic, the peasant, the student. He sought thereby to give work a social and personal content it lacked in the daily lives of these youngsters. All this happened well before Hitler took the labor camps over to be parts of his robot-army.

This kind of labor must not be confused either with the academic scheme of manual training or with the sort of shop experience sometimes provided in engineering schools. I am not speaking of the preparatory phases of education alone; but of the cultivation of the personality throughout life. Our primary concern with this manual discipline should be a humanistic one; its use, the constant reminder of what it takes to be a woman or a man.

Thanks to our pioneer heritage, most Americans have retained a little of this cheerful acceptance of manual tasks: they can wash dishes, putter around a car, or even cook a meal on occasion. But all too easily, they are seduced into a comfortable routine in which these acts are performed for them, by a machine or a hired worker. So their fingers grow clumsy, their muscles slack, their eyes undiscriminating, and their readiness for action disappears

—along with some of their rational judgment and mental balance.

What the personality needs for its integration is not satisfied by a mere hobby, considered as an interest-holding, time-consuming activity. No: active manual labor is all that meets the demand; such labor as the carpenter, the gardener, the woodchopper, the cook, or the cattlehand take part in. The solidarity of workers who have used their hands and shared work experiences is far more real than any abstract solidarity of the so-called working classes. Many of the latter, miserably exploited and sweated, have never had experience of a single day's real work in their lives—work of a personally satisfying nature. All they know is the servile and debasing forms of work: machine-tending, bookkeeping: prisonlike in their bleakness and monotony. Useful labor makes its just demands on everyone; but personal manual labor is the most useful type of all.

39. SOCIAL TEMPERING OF SELF

I come now to a point that has been seriously neglected: the culture of the social man. Here we must correct a weakness that has long been visible and that has almost removed the very underpinnings of democracy. Though in America our schools have made many diverse—but on the whole feeble—attempts to train for citizenship, we have rested too easily content with expanding our purely academic program, or with a damnably iterative emphasis upon the bare concept of democracy.

But we have so far failed to break down the fundamental contradiction that threatens our potential democracy; and that is, the partition between private and public life. We have failed to correct, even symbolically, the state of unbalance that exists between these two phases of the personality. The public be damned is the private motto of the majority of our citizens: which means that they are damning themselves; and at a serious crisis like the present one, they may even be damning themselves to hell, or at least into serfdom.

Now the belief in the sacredness of private property and the romantic belief in the private personality appeared at about the same time. These beliefs were part of that

general gift of privacy which came in with the seventeenth century, and resulted in the private house, the private bedchamber, and private activities generally. This
was a natural outcome, in part, of that politically irresponsible life which was all that was left to the subjects
of an absolute despot, once his privileges as a free citizen
and a member of the guild had been curtailed or entirely
removed.

Even when the republican movement of the eighteenth
century recaptured political responsibility, as it did in the
United States, the habits of privacy tended to persist: they
fitted into the new scheme of private profitmaking. So it
has come about that the major portion of each citizen's
day is still devoted to private activities, his individual
work and his individual family. Indeed, it may even happen that a citizen passes from the cradle to the grave without having performed a single service or a single duty
that would be an earnest of the obligation he owes to the
community that has provided him with all that he has
and is.

As for those who pay perfunctory attention to citizenship, their participation is reserved in the main for
Election Day, while their social service is at best a spo-
radic matter of accepting a call to jury duty or a demand
to serve on a committee for raising charitable funds. Because of this non-participation, because of the popular acceptance of this grossly one-sided arrangement, there is a

large body of ignorant people who even think that the taxes they pay are being exacted from them by a tyrannous government—quite forgetful of all the services and goods those taxes return by way of health, learning, education, safety, and opportunities for co-operative association.

Now the first thing for us to realize is that the type of social economy we are bound to create for the United States, if we are to survive as a nation at all, will demand far more constant political activity on the part of the individual citizen. It is relatively easy for people to accept universal service as a wartime duty, but if our democracy is to remain a healthy, active one, the surrender of "private" time for public duties is likewise indispensable in times of peace. The sole alternative to a repressive regimentation, whether by a personal despot or by an impersonal but equally tyrannical and imbecile "system," is steady, unrelaxing participation in public affairs, by every member of the community. Bosses arise in local politics out of the lethargy and private selfishness of citizens; and they arise on a larger scale, with fascism, for much the same reason, because the habit of accepting the daily burden of political responsibility is not a common one. In any organic democracy, on the contrary, public life must necessarily embrace nearly half of a citizen's existence, day by day, year by year. It cannot be otherwise.

Unless public activity embraces this large area of the personal life, we shall all be subject to a servile absolutism: effective direction will be in the hands of a distant administrative bureaucracy and it will make little difference by what name that bureaucracy is known. Through sheer burden of detail, such a bureaucracy will not be able even to perform its useful functions of co-ordination and standardization: to get the very appearance of co-operation it must sooner or later employ covert or actual coercion. Only the growth of a functional citizenship can avert that breakdown. This applies equally to the running of an industry and to the operation of political government as a whole, for big business is as much enmeshed in red tape as the slowest section of the Circumlocution Office.

But here the great meaning of modern machine production, as a mode of release, as a means of universalizing leisure, appears with all its profound promise. Its meaning does not come mainly from its capacity to supply more goods than ever before. If that were all mankind might exceed its optimum demand and die of overeating, luxury, and boredom. No: the great importance of mechanization derives from the fact that, intelligently used, it should simplify practical life. It should give to Western civilization some of that unharried leisure which older peoples, like the Greeks, got through the labor of slaves.

The mixing of all ranks and classes, all grades of skill

and all manner of aptitudes, all varieties of personality in a military camp—or in a work-camp—is indispensable to a democracy; for only so can it be kept from hardening into castes and factions. But this is only a small part of the effort democracy demands: it asks, not one year's service or five years' service. It must ask for a lifetime of service.

It is only by public work, in which everyone fully participates, that a democracy can be made to operate. This implies more than the performance of military obligations in a crisis; although the readiness to accept such hard, perhaps fatal, compulsions is a necessary phase in the tempering of the human personality. "Muster-day" must come back in a new form, with heavier obligations to drill and exercise and utilize arms: still a guarantee of our liberties until a world order is established.

In short, the public self is no less important than the private self; and it must have its due allotment of time and energy and intelligence. Nor can public duties be performed effectively solely on the initiative of a small group of politicians and public men, no matter how devoted they may be to the commonwealth. They demand the utmost attention, thought, reflection and action by each person.

In each group or community, some will have greater capacities than others; that goes without saying. Those capacities must not be hidden under a show of genial good-fellowship, and an unwillingness to accept more responsibilities than one's neighbors. On the contrary: the acceptance of heavier public burdens is the very essence of an aristocracy; and our democratic system must slump into a fatal mediocrity unless there is a spark of that aristocratic spirit in every village and neighborhood.

False aristocracy seeks privileges, exemptions, ease, special treatment for its class and clique; and the more ruthlessly that kind of aristocracy is wiped out the sounder our country will be. But we cannot dispense with the services of those who have a special vocation for hard jobs. I have met such men, working in complete obscurity, on the Board of Higher Education in New York City: they exist in many quarters and are the very salt of our democracy. That kind of participation must be magnified and extended; and in order to ensure its working, each citizen, both by thought and action, must spend half his time in public life. That goal cannot perhaps be immediately achieved; but it is one to work toward.

40. BEHOLD THE MAN!

There is one final place where the balance of the personality must be restored. This is in the relation of inner to outer activities.

Our whole civilization has become patently extroverted. We ascribe to our thoughts and our feelings, as I have shown, a lower order of reality than we do to physical objects and external organizations. Our capitalistic culture, indeed, was the work of men who had given up the hope of achieving holiness, beatitude, or beauty in order to conquer the forces of nature, master the external world, and roll in their new-found wealth.

The mechanical arts flourished in this transformation; and a large part of human activity, even scholarly research, took on the methods of the mechanical arts. But the work of the humane arts was progressively emptied of social dignity. All that was intimate, personal, non-utilitarian, was regarded by both the business man and the natural scientist as essentially discreditable.

In restoring the balanced personality, capable of giving heed to all the dimensions of human experience, we must displace the power-personality, with its crude one-sided objectives. So it is important, it seems to me, to create a new balance between the inner world and the outer world. Instead of taking the capitalist disparagement of the inner self for granted, and looking upon the concern for it as purely the result of an old-fashioned theology, we must challenge that attitude. We must, to say the least, place no higher value upon fact-finding, acquisition, practical behavior, external activity, than we do upon the inner responses of contemplation, fantasy building, evaluation, and expression.

The great task of the expressive arts—and in another fashion the great task of religion—is to socialize this otherwise private inner world, to unite it with its heritage of durable values, and finally to bring it into the open and project it in new forms quick with meaning for other men.

During the last century we have done much to build up the orderly, rational, fact-finding, emotionally equable personality. We have rigorously trained people to displace their emotional reactions, to overcome their ingrained prejudices in dealing with repulsive materials or processes, to sacrifice their pet wishes, to conceal their desires. We have done this so well that even the man in the street is prepared to look upon any spectacle, no matter how horrible, and to tolerate it meekly, no matter how sharply it calls for correction. We have done our job all too well. We have created on an unbelievable scale people who accept with becoming impotence the objective conditions laid down by nature and society.

But there is a sense in which this emotionless moral neutrality has come to be a terrible sterilizing device. Even apart from those issues that I discussed in dealing with the weaknesses of pragmatic liberalism, this device has proved an effective block to creative expression and confident constructive activity. The hysterical protest of fascism against any sort of objectivity, its raucous emphasis of the most primitive emotions, are in a sense pathological efforts to overcome one of the real curses of modern civilization: the disbelief in the inner man. The fascist's misbehavior is an irrational protest against the false dogmas of "behaviorism."

Those who are most adept in displacing themselves lack precisely the emotional impetus that gives rise to new goals and new fulfillments not provided in the immediate situation. That is to say, they are completely without imagination; and this, perhaps, is why they have been so pathetically bewildered and helpless in attempting to meet the assaults of manic but imaginative men. Such neutralized persons regard the will-to-create as essentially immodest. Aware of all the tangled intellectual complexities that fact-finding reveals, desiring to know rather than to do, these passive individuals distrust the quick syntheses and the brilliant shortcuts that the artist in any vocation always makes in proceeding from reflection to action.

For these hopeless neutrals there is an air of impudence, even of charlatanry, in the characteristic habits of the painter, the architect, or the statesman; for the latter, if they are good at all, always have the capacity for acting on insufficient evidence and for building better than they know. Their actions not merely speak louder than their words, but they speak more to the point.

In the political field, then, some of the strength of fascism undoubtedly derives from its legitimate criticism of the feeble desires, the deepseated self-distrust, that this neutral type of personality—the very paragon of the gentlemanly academic virtues—exhibits when faced with responsibility for action of any kind. Only forceful dreamers can cut through routine.

Here is why religion and the expressive arts have a particular message for our generation; for they have never abandoned the cultivation of the self; and they have done this by methods that are generally valid, not those which promote mental unbalance and corruption. Plainly, a great part of the work that must be done during the next century, by way of either salvage or construction, is of a formative nature: old routines will provide no guide to it. Mere knowledge, mere fact-finding, mere statistical analysis, mere technical skill will not lead to these new forms: such qualities can lead only to some minor modification of past forms—and as every intelligent mind now knows, the latter are doomed, and small modifications will not save them.

If our social order is to become deeply creative—if it is even to be good enough to improvise a system of military strategy that will meet the unexpected—it will necessarily be the work of people who have a robust inner life: confidence in the validity of their dreams and projects. We have had enough ducking and deprecating and side-stepping; and more than enough routineering.

Our salvation will lie in giving a major opportunity to the creative people and in cultivating more of them: people who are capable of adapting social forms to social needs as completely as an artist is capable of creating, out of the chaos of experience, a painting, a poem, or a symphony. Subjective confidence should not be the monopoly of raging paranoiacs: its normal expression is the very quality of the artist.

One final sphere of self-fulfillment remains, beyond that of emotional stimulus, manual discipline, public service, and creative expression. This is the deliberate cultivation of the inner life by withdrawal, purposive contemplation, and self-communion. Such cultivation is the most precious part of every religion. Patrick Geddes in his theory of the cloister, as later A. J. Toynbee in his theory of withdrawal-and-return, has shown it to have an indispensable place in the social process. From Ignatius Loyola to Nicolai Lenin, from Benedict of Nursia to Hitler, those who have made the deepest impression upon their age are those who

300

have first plumbed their own depths—in prison, in exile, on the sickbed, or in deliberate retreat.

Without this withdrawal, the pieties of the religious too easily become platitudes; and their vision of the universe remains a tepid one. It is alone, in the wilderness or in the cell, that men re-make their destiny. In the midst of the present apocalypse of violence, one cannot hope that the synthesis of cults and creeds, of cosmologies and sciences, that must ultimately be demanded for modern man will take place in time to alter the present posture of affairs. Too much must be discarded; too many stones for the new building are still unquarried.

But one thing is possible to unite all who dream of a larger human co-operation and a wider synthesis; and this is the renewal of the habit of contemplation itself. A half hour a day, at least, in solitude: free from all calls or interruptions—alone, as the saying used to be, with one's God. Such a habit, if widely practiced, might do more to promote poise and fortitude than the filling of the pews in all the churches. Above all, it would quicken the imagination. Without a renewal of the inner vision, there can be no firm attack upon our practical difficulties.

In those quiet moments of apartness, the self may find itself once more in communion with other selves: an underlying common ground, unspeakable and unspoken, for both personality and community. Composed and collected, aware of its present position, no matter how terrible, and its ultimate goals, no matter how remote, the self may return with swift assured steps to society. Fortified. Unafraid of the burdens of life, undismayed by the oncoming of barbaric terror or the prospects of death. Fortified. Ready to die or live.

PART SEVEN:

Sacrifice and Salvage

All hands save ship! has startled dreamers.

HERMAN MELVILLE

41. ALL HANDS SAVE SHIP!

When a ship is battling through a storm of hurricane violence and has sprung leaks that the pumps cannot keep up with, there is sometimes one chance of keeping it afloat: throwing overboard its heavy cargo. No matter how precious that cargo may be, its weight may cause the ship to sink. If it is to ride the storm and save the lives aboard, Captain and crew must, with quick zeal, throw overboard all those things which, in calmer weather, might have been brought to their destination. And when the call, "All hands save ship!" is given, everyone must drop his familiar routine and bear a hand. At that moment all private choices vanish.

Plainly we are now in the midst of such a storm; and plainly, too, our ship is a leaky one. We would like to save everything that we value in our civilization, the small dear toys of our children no less than the canister of food, the deck-chairs we relaxed in no less than our life-belts. But the inexorable conditions we face will not permit it. We must save what is most worth saving, that which will ultimately serve our humanity, that which will guarantee that our children will have toys again, and the aged a place where they may quietly stretch their feet.

305

In short: we must save the vessel itself; our civilization and the institutions and habits of free men. Some day our children, perhaps only our great-grandchildren, will find a safe anchorage in quiet waters, within sight of a green coast and white buildings, and the sea-gulls circling and the smell of grass floating over the waters.

This saying is harder than the figure of the storm-tossed vessel indicates; unless one remembers that those who stick to their posts in a storm to work the vessel may be caught in an avalanche of water and swept overboard. Unless they stick to their posts, no matter what cold terrors they face, the boat will sink. For we cannot do our job if we seek first to save our lives or even to protect our children's lives, once they are old enough to take their turn at the watch. We cannot save bodies. We can only save the spirit that makes those bodies significant.

In the long run it will not matter for humanity if London is ruined as completely as the heart of Rotterdam, provided that those who die in the ruins pass on to the survivors the spirit that is capable of building a greater London. Nothing whatever is saved if only the bodies and the buildings are saved: to crumble stone by stone; to die, drop by drop.

Similarly, nothing is lost if the spirit lives; for a little leaven will leaven the whole loaf. It is not those who sought safety first or who surrendered quickest who will carry on the work of our civilization. It is those who barely escaped with their lives, the Czechs who continued the struggle, the Poles, the Norwegians, the French, above all, the brave British who continued to fight. As for the rest, most of them were, pitiably, the appointed victims of fascism because they thought that their material goods mattered and their bodies were worth keeping alive. That is the conviction of corpses: to that degree, the most brutal fascist who risked his life was still a better man.

What we need, to get to port finally, is the ship itself, a few hands to navigate it, and above all the compass, the chart, the chronometer to give us our bearings. Nothing else matters perhaps. And if the violence and carnage spread, nothing else can be saved. We cannot preserve ourselves against this barbarism and worry about the cost of our effort: we must give beyond the ordinary power of giving. Nor can we ensure seven per cent profits or the eventual redemption of all our bonds and mortgages at par value; nor can we hold fast to a particular patent monopoly or a particular hourly wage scale. Only one need counts: the need to save the institutions of a free civilization, the institutions of democracy, founded on a profound respect for the personality of all men, and for a power, not ourselves, that makes for righteousness.

Too late in the war the British and the French discovered how great a sacrifice the danger demanded: the French were unprepared for it until all they valued was indeed churned around and pounded to pieces in the beating waters; until the plates were buckling and the water swamping the hold. The ruling classes thought of an easy, circumspect triumph, which would keep all their snug securities, their imperial monopolies, their colonies, their landed and City interests functioning as always before for the convenience and comfort of these classes. American business men—at least a very vocal minority—are still making the same mistake: some are even toying with the earliest of Chamberlain's fatal stupidities, that of making a deal with the fascists, on Chamberlain's very assumption, that after all "we must live in the same world." Intelligence that has decayed so far is almost liquid with putrefaction.

Too late the sleek English rulers discovered, as men discover when they take to the lifeboats, that the first-class passenger who has occupied the royal suite has no better chance of surviving than the poor waif from a third-class bunk: that in fact to save their lives those who had once been treated with punctilio must relinquish all thought of place and position and wealth and take their chances with the ship's company, living on hardtack and water, having even their private flask or private spirit lamp commandeered by the boatswain, in order to give every member of the boat a fighting chance.

We in America shall not work swiftly enough, ruthlessly enough, nor shall we have the means of striking back against fascism hard enough, if we think we can baby ourselves through this crisis. We are working against a barbarian power that has demanded and exacted years of bitter sacrifice from every man, woman, and child in Germany, if one excepts of course the fat Goerings and the sleek Hitlers for whose perverse dreams the sacrifice has been enacted. Fascism's power is great just in proportion to the unwillingness, on the side of the nations they threaten, to depart from their comfortable bourgeois routine. Mr. Walter Lippmann has well called those who think that they must give up no vested interest or privilege whatever, the sleepwalkers; and that is the most charitable name one could apply. Some of these Rip Van Winkles fell asleep before 1933.

The mistakes of Europe, above all, the mistakes of France and England, are a warning to us who survive: *if we cling to the cargo we may lose the ship.* We must strip for action. Nothing is sacred except our ship—our democracy itself—the civilization we share with all men of good will—the ideals that have shaped us—the heritage of immaterial things we hope to hand on to our children. We Americans must struggle for democracy—that is progress, experiment, adventure, innovation: a ceaseless war that brings no promise of security, a war of the spirit against the Caliban in man and old Chaos in nature: a war of the spirit against all that obstructs spirit. Fascism promises peace: *fascist peace, which is death.* While democracy lives, that is the one kind of peace we will spurn to accept.

42. THE ECONOMICS OF SACRIFICE

This book intentionally reverses the usual order of political writings. Usually they begin with a specific indictment of abuses and go on to detail various measures for correcting them. At the end, they perhaps include some vague allusion to culture or the higher life, taking for granted that everyone agrees on these matters of value—and that if they do not it will not signify much.

In contrast, this book has been concerned with first and last things. The reader who has followed my argument and accepted the philosophy behind it, could write these last chapters without my help. My procedure has of course been deliberate; based on the belief that some common agreement as to what life means, what is worth living for, and for what, in extremity, one must die quite cheerfully is the first step to a restored national morale. Without such an underlying agreement, our actual political moves will be chickenhearted and ineffective: we will, in fact, be ruled by the same sort of financial and political defectives, scoring little points in debate, protecting this interest, sliding into that office, cadging that favor, who brought democratic Europe to calamity.

But I would not make the mistake of leaving the argument at this point. For our present situation has created many practical problems that must be met, and that can be met only if we move swiftly from faith to rational conviction, and from conviction to action. In practical life, the change needed is quite as drastic as any suggestions I have made for the personal life. Briefly, our present danger demands a transfer of loyalty from an economics of comfort to an economics of sacrifice.

This change will bear lightest on the poor and the insecure, the unemployed and the unskilled; for they have, willy-nilly, lived under an economics of sacrifice, and will have their turn at last to improve their condition, through the very fact that no one's services can be spared, and no human claim must be left disregarded. But the change will fall hard on the rich and the middle class. No matter how zealously they may think of themselves as Christians, they bow in prayer with a soft cushion under their knees, and they do not really expect to have to renounce their dear possessions until the day of judgment. All their views call for swift revisions: only those who met a similar demand in the bankruptcy of the last depression will at first be capable of making the transfer.

But they will not be alone in their reluctance; they will not lack company when they make excuses. Most Americans, even the working class, are starkly unprepared for this change. That is why they cling so fatuously to the notion of peace or at least of a system of defense that will involve no risk—as if there were any Chinese walls that would keep out the present barbarians, or as if cowering behind a few pitiful military barriers and waiting for the blow to strike will not be the very state that would give success to our enemies.

During the last two decades Americans have quaintly persuaded themselves that they live under an economy of abundance; even the poor believe that. One and all they have looked forward to enlarging their possessions; and they have usually copied the habits of the economic class just above them, vicariously participated in them at the cinema; and envied them when they were not able to go quite so far. "Haven't I got a right to a car?" "Haven't I got a right to a new suite of furniture?" These are the questions asked by the pathetic starvelings in a recent novel: a study of a family on relief.

And the answer now, to rich and poor, must be a firm one. The only right anyone has as an American is to an equal share in the good life. Not a life of material abundance; but a life of comradeship, art, and love. Comradeship, art, and love are outside the market; one cannot call them either cheap or dear. But in the days to come comradeship, art, and love are all that we shall be able to offer honestly to those who take part in the sacrifice, to those who stick to their posts, wherever they are, to those who give up their dearest habits and their dearest possessions for the preservation of our democracy. These gifts are on the same level; and they alone are capable of sweetening the sacrifice. Lovers will know what I mean; and for all decent parents it is ancient wisdom.

The economy of sacrifice turns the economy of comfort upside down: minus becomes plus and vice-versa. Our new economy must assume that hardship, difficulty, and poverty are normal aspects of life; that everything above that level, for our generation, is a piece of unqualified good luck, to be valued for what it is, a rare and exceptional thing, not to be demanded as a right. Poverty, hardship, wounds, and death will be our daily pay.

Without this transvaluation of our existing economic values, we shall not even have the physical means of survival. For the only abundance that our skill with machines will create will be an abundance of weapons, munitions, tanks, airplanes, warships, or still undreamed-of pieces of armament; all horrible to contemplate, all expensive to produce. To create these weapons on the scale necessary to defend ourselves, and to clothe and feed those who use them, while they perform no compensating industrial work, cannot be done except by paring down to the bone on every other item of consumption.

There can, of course, be no holding back because of the expense or the load of the debt; only those who prefer slavery to freedom and fascism to democracy would have us hold back. If a four-shift day in industry, six hours to the worker, will provide a greater amount of munitions more quickly than a three-shift day, we must be ready, at least in the immediate crisis, to introduce it. And there can be no holding back lest we upset "normal arrangements."

Or again: should the defense of New York require the immediate provision of deep underground airdromes it might be necessary to stop running the West Side Subway above 181st Street and clear all the apartment houses away around Dyckman Street, in order to use the subway for an airdrome and the space in front as a landing field. I use this merely as an example, not as a proposal; an example to show how drastic and absolute must be our willingness to tear into established habits of life. In any department where action is needed, we must be able to think in this untrammeled, relentless fashion.

Or take another illustration, also not a proposal. Millions of dollars go every year into the cosmetics and chewing gum industries in the United States. In order to have a sufficient number of workers, machines, and factories for all the accessory war industries—since armies and navies do not live by bullets alone—it may be necessary to let every girl's face remain unrouged, unpowdered, unperfumed. While to provide sufficient food for ourselves and our surviving partners in the fight—if indeed we have any allies left at that terrible moment—half the fields that are now cultivated for tobacco may have to be turned over to the production of food.

314

From the standpoint of the economy of comfort, all these changes are worse than devastating; they are quite unthinkable. That is why our country must switch to an economy of sacrifice, under which the only unthinkable thing would be putting time and energy into the production of goods that do not serve either to increase the chances of survival or to augment the human heritage we seek to pass on to the next generation. Money for scientific research and responsible scholarship, yes—more than ever; but for competitive advertising, for pulp magazines, high bred dog kennels—no.

The same rule applies to all the new work that must be done to provide houses and communities for the expanded munitions industries; for the precedents that have so far been established—except perhaps in the subsistence homestead projects and migratory workers' camps—must be scrapped. We must provide hundreds of thousands of new homes for the new war workers, first to give them an extra stake in their land, and second to decrease the labor-turnover. Not merely must they have real houses, not shacks or barracks; but in the vital matter of domestic and communal space, we must provide gardens, schools, meeting rooms, libraries, open areas for agriculture and recreation; facilities on a scale better than all but the best today.

To do this is merely an act of social justice; it is also a guarantee of health, content, working efficiency; it will raise the birth rate, probably, and lower the need for medical treatment: both important. But when I say better I do not mean more elaborate or more expensive. Just the contrary. Where wood or coal is cheap the open fireplace may replace central heating; modern methods of insulation and modern discoveries in orientation for sunlight make this feasible, even in the colder parts of the country. We shall very probably need the steamfitters, the radiator makers, the boiler makers, the motor fabricators, for other purposes. So, too, these houses may have to forego electric refrigerators; a cold closet and an infant's ice chest will perhaps be all we can afford.

The rule is plain: provide everything that is essential for *life;* but nothing beyond that; nothing for sale, for show, for imitative expenditure of the class above, or for making it easier to sell the quarters to a higher bidder when the struggle is over. During these years of sacrifice, it may well be that there will be a wider distribution of oranges; but fewer provisions for making ice-cubes or frozen desserts. On the other hand, it is essential that a school, a library, a community meeting room be provided with every new neighborhood development: those, too, are vital to the personality and essential to the transmission of our democratic heritage.

We can spare electric refrigerators if we have to; but we cannot spare books. We may have to forego new motor cars for years at a time; but we must not forego the services of competently trained teachers, or forget the continued revitalization of the mind through scholarship, science, and works of the imagination. We can do without costly arterial parkways and vast amusement grounds that divert the metropolitan populace from the realities of living; but we cannot do without higher education in all its branches, in all its refinements.

In other words we must reverse the crazy economy we once held so sacred: the economy we carried on even during the bitter days of the depression. In New York, for example, the municipality put millions of dollars into new bridges, parkways, and new arterial avenues. Meanwhile, many of its schools were overcrowded and underequipped; likewise its foremost municipal college.

All this was done under an exceptionally able Mayor, the best, probably, that ever held office in the city. It was done, not out of perversity, but because an economy of comfort demands spectacular expenditures, which make life easier or smoother or brighter for the middle classes. Under an economy of sacrifice, just the opposite principle prevails: material improvements are not paramount but subordinate; instruments of human purpose.

The economy of sacrifice promises art, comradeship, and love; all these freely and abundantly. Those who enter its service are entitled to these things no matter what their previous standing in the community; even the rich may share in this boon. If they have ability, their talents will be employed to the full, with dignity, with

317

the respect and co-operation of every fellow worker; but their reward, like that of the least of us, will be a nominal one. All that is represented by vast private estates, private art collections, yachts, fleets of motor cars, expensive coming-out parties, private luxury and private amusement, will vanish. These things will vanish because they were founded upon power and privilege, not on justice; vanish not only because they are not worth saving, but because it would be indecent and immoral to retain them, except in a relation of bare custodianship, till some more permanent disposition is made, while the rest of the community is grinding its life to the bone.

Our industrial system in the present crisis must effect a revolution from within, for the necessary changes cannot be made swiftly and surely enough through mere outside pressure. The organizers and directors of this system must take over the classic tradition of the professional classes: public service and public responsibility. We do not bestow our judgeships on the highest bidder or turn over our army to the general who promises to give himself and his staff the biggest rakeoff. On the contrary, these people work at fixed salaries, within the same general range of reward. It is nothing short of dishonorable in a democracy for the president of a private corporation to get a higher salary than the President of the United States; and the same principle holds all down the line.

Now there are a certain number of business men, indus-

318

trialists, and technicians who are ready for this re-orientation. They have labored within the framework of capitalism because that system trained them and gave them their opportunities. But they are primarily interested in getting the work done and in having the authority and the power to do it. Their fun lies in the doing more than in the reward.

Some of these men lost their fortunes in 1929 and started again from the ground up; and now that their country's peril exposes them to an even sterner reality, they will not flinch. There is enough of the pioneer in them to make them ready for this new game, in which the old poker chips will not be used to count the winnings. Such industrial pioneers are matched by a small group of labor leaders of equal capabilities.

Upon the willingness of such leaders to reconstruct our whole industrial fabric, to make it capable of full production and well-apportioned consumption, our very salvation during the next few years may depend. There are plainly only a handful of people like this: the majority of business men have only timid, selfish, fashionable minds, and they are abetted by an anti-social minority headed by the egregious Henry Ford. But the more dynamic and public-spirited leaders have an opportunity for service that few statesmen have ever had; and if they answer the call, there will be public authority to back their best efforts. In a day that calls for a hard, driving discipline, the first place to curtail luxuries, to minimize extravagances, and to lessen pecuniary rewards is in the upper reaches of industry itself. If there is not healthy patriotism and sacrifice at that point, there will be only suspicion and hatred in the lower ranks—not undeserved suspicion, not unprovoked hatred.

If the worker gives up the right to strike during this emergency, the government must not merely provide a local administrative agency to ensure justice; for that in outline already exists. The worker and the farmer must have the assurance that the sacrifices that are demanded of them bear equally on all. Previous conveniences and previous habits of life that have become second nature must go by the board. The inner acceptance of this condition will make the surrender easier; but easy or hard, an economy of sacrifice is needed. Under this economy all business, whether directly serving the war or not, whether in private hands or under public management, will be run primarily for the wealth and welfare of the American people, and for the honor and dignity of the civilization we uphold.

On our capacity for making this sacrifice, almost before these words are printed, depends the very possibility of our survival as a free people. It is a drastic demand; but it carries with it a great promise. And that is the promise, through the desperate effort itself, of achieving a swift measure of social regeneration. The war will not be utopia; far from it; nor will that which survives it, if anything survives, be any easy way of living. Nor will our present sacrifices make further sacrifices unnecessary. They have a higher mission than this: they will make them meaningful.

43. THE POLITICS OF SACRIFICE

What applies in the realm of economics applies equally in the realm of politics; for there is a politics of sacrifice.

Up to now our political institutions have reflected the vice of our other social forms: we have had a politics of comfort, in which people enjoyed privileges without responsibilities, and exercised liberties without performing duties. This applies to nations no less than individuals; there is scarcely a judgment one can make about one that does not hold for the other; and Machiavelli's assumption of the contrary to this is the very impulse that has helped to make peoples, collectively, more vicious than the greater part of them are personally and individually.

Under the old conception of national sovereignty the sacred egoism of the state, to use one of the bombastic epithets of the fascists, has been paramount. So long as states regarded themselves as sovereign and therefore irresponsible they made impossible any lasting comity between their peoples. Each state believed in right, law, justice, only as long as it was permitted to have its own way. A criminal believes in law and right on those terms.

The first principle that a politics of sacrifice must establish in the mind of each citizen is that his precious heritage

322

of freedom and self-government are conditional: his self-government depends upon his personal participation in all the processes of political action; in his trade union or his farmers' co-operative no less than in his municipal elections. No withdrawal of interest from government is possible without giving the privilege of unqualified control to those who will make evil use of it. A crooked trade union leader is a large step toward a crooked fascist leader.

Much the same applies to national governments. The politics of sacrifice will reverse the injustices of imperialism, as the United States, to the honor of its citizens, has done in the case of both Cuba and the Philippines. There is no double standard of freedom; if the peoples of Polynesia or Africa are not to be left in a state of abject barbarism nor exploited for the gain of other peoples, even provisional aid to them must be on a partnership basis. The failure to establish this relation has given a bad conscience to Great Britain with respect to India; and it is the source of the British Empire's strength with respect to the Dominions.

An English liberal politician once said, in words that express the absolute difference between democracy and despotism, "Good government is no substitute for self-government." Which is another way of expressing the essential theological dogma of the Christian Church: free will, the power to go wrong, is the foundation of both high morality and high politics.

As with individual freedom, national freedom belongs only to those who are peacefully disposed. Freedom for the individual does not give him the privilege to brandish a gun in the public thoroughfare, or to exact tribute from his neighbor by blackmail; nor does it permit the criminally insane to remain at large, ready to commit rape, arson, or murder, because they fancy themselves the Emperors of the World. We must accept the fact of human conflict and seek to adjust by peaceful measures the most vital differences between people or groups; freedom rests, therefore, on a body of law, on courts of justice, upon a police force, if necessary a whole army, capable of bringing the offender to book if he persists in his offense or defies the law. Most of all, national freedom rests, therefore, on the re-establishment of common moral standards for our whole civilization.

There will be no possibility of orderly conflict between human groups until similar measures are enforced for each state and community. Disarmament by itself is no guarantee of security or law; indeed the farther it goes, the more chance there is for the cunning and the violent, with relatively little effort, to seize power, and monopolize it, at the expense of a disarmed world. Disarmament without law is an invitation to brigandage: the most futile kind of sacrifice.

For who is so naive as to think that there will come a time in international affairs when the powerful will not seek to exert power and the violent will not seek by violence to impose their will upon the timid? Such a moment has never yet come in the affairs of individual citizens, over any great area of space and time. For power is a permanent fact in political life; and it is only in heaven that good intentions will prevail without the authoritative use of force. What makes civil life tolerable in non-fascist countries without a daily dose of terror and anxiety is that in such countries strife and conflict have been moralized and have orderly channels of expression.

The politics of sacrifice demands, as the price of living in an orderly world, the unqualified surrender of so-called national sovereignty to a higher authority, acting under a common constitution and law, in which all the states that participate shall have a part. Without such a renunciation of power by the democratic states, as between themselves, they can never be free from perils like those that are now ruining life for hundreds of millions of simple men and women. In short, the state must sacrifice what old-fashioned legists used to regard as the very essence of statehood.

This politics of sacrifice may seem a long way off, since there will be no means of creating it for the world at large until fascism crumbles. But it has very direct economic and social implications today; and the sooner we face them the better. Apart from the one-sided domination of Africa and Asia by the European, the most cry-ing injustice on the international stage comes from the maldistribution of natural resources: partly due to nature, partly to privileged monopolies. There are two ways of overcoming this injustice. One is by inventing artificial equivalents of these natural resources or products: artificial rubber from petroleum, for example; or sun motors instead of coal for the tropics: sun hot water heaters already exist. The other is by pooling and sharing these resources.

For the fact is that even from the most narrowly technical standpoint, a high and resourceful economy must draw upon the whole world for sustenance, just as it must draw upon the whole world for scientific and inventive ideas. Take a highly advanced instrument like the telephone: its refinement is based upon the use of chromium and cobalt in making permanent magnets. These elements come from Rhodesia, the Soviet Union, South Africa, and Turkey. Nickel is another component: 85 per cent of it comes from Canada. Antimony is still another: this metal comes from China, Belgium, and Mexico. And so it goes. The same holds true, as Professor Eugene Staley has shown in "This Shrinking World," for the two hundred different materials that go into a modern motor car.

Only technological illiterates can imagine that a national or even a continental economy would guarantee life except on an exceedingly primitive industrial basis. If ever the fascists should seize the major part of the planet, whilst we cringed behind our own frontiers, we should find that we no longer had the physical means to resist them, for every gun and machine we made would, ultimately, be inferior to theirs, and about as capable of competing with them as a home-made automobile compared with a Rolls-Royce.

Mechanical invention, as I have said elsewhere, is no substitute for justice; and international justice demands the creation of a worldwide authority for the allocation and distribution of power and raw materials. Even while fighting the fascists, the beginnings of such a distribution must be made by the democratic survivors. Such an authority would iron out inequalities; even fix quantities in advance of production. All the details would be intricate and difficult to work out; but the alternative is ruinous.

This is the economic basis for that human brotherhood which our world-encircling radios and world-girdling airplanes have thus far turned mainly into an insane mockery. The weight of power and opportunity is never of course equal; so no World Authority could give to a group of forlorn Eskimos near the Arctic Circle the same advantages that a group of equally worthy men would have if they were close to libraries and universities and factories and power houses. But justice works at least in the direction of equalization. Under a politics of sacrifice, those nations who up to now have esteemed themselves as most independent, most wealthy, and most sovereign must make the major act of sharing and giving, for the benefit of the rest of mankind.

Mere survival will dictate as much in the starving world we shall perhaps face within a year: first for agricultural commodities and later for capital resources. This step involves a drastic redirection in our methods of thinking; and worst of all, the greatest change is needed among the most benighted part of our population, democratic statesmen cadging for office, short-sighted and self-important, inflating their own bladderlike egos with their country's prestige. But if free peoples must be prepared to give up their lives in defense of civilization, they should be somewhat more ready to give up their prejudices.

The politics of sacrifice imposes a further duty on the people of the United States. No other country has a past with respect to other nations and races that is both so shabby and so glorious. In our treatment of the Indian and the Negro our record is as sullied as the most rapacious and brutal European power. No patriotic American would defend anything about our conduct here except our belated efforts at restitution and justice.

But at the same time, when our country was young and our confidence in ourselves still clean and vigorous, we opened our land up to the refugees and willing immigrants from every country in the world. There was a dark side to this generosity; we needed more people in order to be strong and wealthy, and we exploited mercilessly, by turn, each new garnering of muscle and brawn. Nevertheless, nothing can diminish the luster of the larger gift: we gave them land and the institutions of freedom. Until the eighties, we took in even the pauper, the sick, the criminal; so easygoing and all-embracing was our gesture.

This generosity had a noble compensation. The United States of America became in effect the United States of Europe. We have been, in our own right, an embodiment of that more friendly order we must now seek to bring about throughout the planet; we know its advantages, and we have had experience of its difficulties, too. Today the very need of our democracy for sheer weight of numbers to ensure our survival, if fascism keeps alive for as much as a decade without breaking down or alternatively demolishing us—this need suggests a return to our earlier doctrines and beliefs.

We need more newcomers by birth. We need them also by immigration; and should be prepared at the least, in these times of misery and starvation, to take in a million refugees a year, as we did in better days. If we wish to have the right to survive the fascist aggression, let us accept this sacrifice as a sacred duty. The task will not be easy; nothing today that is worth doing is easy. Plainly, it would be extremely difficult even in times of peace. But our sacrifice will be small, in comparison with what those who resisted have suffered, and in comparison with the widening circles of misery around us.

The United States, with its federal system of government and its strong centralized executive, is an image of the greater world we must help create for all men. That is the vital core of Clarence Streit's case for Union Now. His weakness is that he assumes this union possible without a politics and an economics of sacrifice: forgetful of the fact that the comfortable will sacrifice nothing that lessens their comfort—not even their illusions.

All these demands for political sacrifice must have an unfamiliar sound. That is because they are based on an indisputable fact; namely, we are living in an unfamiliar world; and we shall never emerge from it safely if we cling cravenly to old formulas or attempt to hide behind mildewed prejudices. Those who think that we democratic peoples can keep any life that is worth having without risking it a dozen times over are still walking in their sleep. No sacrifice of sovereignty or self-sufficiency or self-complacency can be too great, if it enables us to keep alive.

44. LAST TESTAMENT

I have made no attempt to trim this argument to meet the objections of those who do not know that a thousand years separates 1940 from 1930; they are hopeless. I appeal only to those who realize that we Americans are already among the last stout survivors on a sinking ship. I appeal only to those who love life, but are willing to face death so that life may go on. I appeal to those who have experienced love, but who know that no smaller love than that of humanity will enable the love of mates and friends to be secure. I appeal only to those who still carry on the tradition of immigrants and pioneers: those who dared much to create a new world. The task our ancestors started is not finished. The struggle is not over. We have a job to do, the hardest that ever faced a generation; harder still because it was sprung suddenly on us, and we have scarcely time to get our bearings before we plunge into it. Our job is to restore our own faith for living, and to lay the foundations of a world in which life—love, freedom, justice, truth—will once more be sacred.

If we rise to the task, we will have our good moments; the sacrifice will not be unrelieved. Though much will be snatched from us that is still precious, the moments that remain will be keener because of the very threat that they may be near our last. Parents will turn with a new devotion to their children, husband to wife, sister to brother, neighbor to neighbor. That feeling awakens in a shipwreck and sometimes survives the wreckage.

Nothing is sure; not death, not victory. Because we have a deep corruption to throw off in ourselves as well as our community before we are fit to fight; because we awakened belatedly and have only partial, sleepy energies to use at first, we may even be beaten. But that is no reason for flinching or for bowing beforehand to defeat. To those who would abandon the very hope of struggle I would repeat the counsel that Krishna offered Arjuna on the eve of battle, as told in the Bhagavad-Gita. Like the slack liberals, the pacifists, the wormy business men, the shirking politicians, Arjuna hesitated, debated, had specious moral scruples, clung to the hope of safety in a situation that did not permit him to enjoy it. Victory, Krishna pointed out, is never guaranteed beforehand. What is important for man is to attend to the overwhelming duty of the moment, in a spirit of emancipated understanding. "Counting gain or loss as one, prepare for battle!"

Counting gain or loss as one, knowing that gains are losses and losses are often gains: there lies a truth to take us through these hard days. In that spirit, only in that spirit, can our civilization be saved.

Man's destiny is a great one because the essence of it is tragic. All that he builds crumbles; all that he embodies turns to dust; all that he loves most, he must one day leave behind him. That which alone endures on earth is the spirit in which he understands and meets his fate. This he passes on to his children and his comrades: only a breath indeed, but the breath of life. Death comes to all; but death comes best to those who are ready to die, so that Man may live. The words of Jesus are ultimate in their wisdom: "He that loseth his life shall find it."

That applies to individual men; it applies to nations and peoples. No smaller faith will console us for temporary defeats, sustain us in the hours of despair, or give us the strength to push through to victory.

THE END